Healing Power of Gems

Dr. Gopal Sharma
Pr. Sewaram Jaipuria

Lotus PRESS
4735/22, Prakash Deep Building
Ansari Road, Darya Ganj,
New Delhi - 110002

Lotus Press : Publishers & Distributors
Unit No. 220, 2nd Floor, 4735/22, Prakash Deep Building,
Ansari Road, Darya Ganj, New Delhi- 110002
Ph.: 23280047, 98118-38000
• E-mail : lotuspress1984@gmail.com
www.lotuspress.co.in

Healing Power of Gems

ISBN: 81-8382-114-6

Printed & Published by : **Lotus Press Publisher & Distributors,** New Delhi-02

Preface

The present treatise is a brilliant attempt by Dr. Gopal Sharma, Vice-President All India Federation of Astrologer's Societies & Pracharya Sewaram Jaipuria, Principal Institute of Vaastu & Joyful Living explaining the origin, characteristics and healing powers of precious/ semi precious gemstones. I sincerely hope that this information will be very useful for people in all walks of life. Wishing the learned authors all success in their future endeavors.

—Vibha Aggarwal

Prof. Indian Gemological Institute

Gem Testing Laboratory

Jhandewallan, New Delhi

Acknowledgement

Besides all the ancient and modern scholars our deep gratitude and sincere thanks are due to Ms. **Vibha Aggarwal,** Professor in Gemology in Indian Gemological Institute, Gem Testing Laboratory, Jhandewalan run by Gem & Jewellery Export Promotion Council New Delhi, who has enlightened us with infinite knowledge and experience. Her moral support and cooperation was extremely valuable to us in preparation of this book.

Our friends, admirers, clients, & readers, innumerable increasing letters also helped us in compiling this book for which we are grateful to all of them.

We are especially indebted to Er. **H. Ahuja** and Sh. **Vind Goel** who devoted a lot of time for material research and editing, leaving aside their own work.

We are also thankful to Sh. **Gagan Aggarwal** President **Aadi Shankaracharya** Vedic Education Society & Rt. **O.P. Bhardwaj** for their inspiration and encouragement to present this book in its beautiful get up for the enlightened readers.

We express our sincere thanks to Sh. **A.J. Sehgal,** Director Lotus Press without whose continous efforts presentation of this treatise would not have been possible.

Pracharaya Sewa Ram Jaipuria | *Dr. Gopal Sharma*

Contents

Books By Same Authors

1. मोक्ष वाटिका 50/-
2. लक्ष्मी प्रवेश कैसे हो ? 60/-
3. सुगम वास्तुशास्त्र 75/-
4. प्रगतिशील वास्तु 195/-
5. श्री साई गृह वास्तु सूत्र 120/-
6. सफल जीवन में अंकों का महत्व 75/-
7. चमत्कारिक लक्ष्मी यंत्र (अंकों का खजाना) 125/-
8. जानिए भविष्य आई–चिंग द्वारा एवं द्वार का प्रभाव 60/-
9. सुख का आधार वास्तु द्वारा सुधार बिना तोड़े–फोड़ 30/-
10. जानिए उपचार पायरा वास्तु तथा फेंग–हुई द्वारा 90/-
11. समृद्धि और सफलता के 108 सुनहरी उपाय 90/-
12. Advance Feng-shui 195/-
13. Progressive Vaastu 225/-
14. Wonders Of Numbers 60/-
15. Comprehensive Vaastu 75/-
16. Pyramid Power & Vaastu 195/-
17. Science Of Gruha Vaastu 195/-
18. Vaastu Correction Without Demolition 95/-
19. Sri Sai Science Of Gruha Vaastu Model Plans 350/-
20. The Secrets Of A Happy Life Through Pyra-Vaastu & Feng-shui 90/-
21. The Magic Loshu Grid (Treasure Of Numbers) 260/-
22. Teach Yourself Vaastu 150/-
23. 108 Golden Tips For Love, Health, Wealth & Success 90/-
24. The Rationale Behind Indian Rituals & Beliefs 168/-
25. Advance Interior Designing Incorporating Vaastu & Feng-shui 90/-
26. Teach yourself Astrology 125/-
27. Teach yourself Numerology 125/-
28. Learn Meditation 125/-
29. Awake Kundalini 125/-
30. Teach yourself Graphology 150/-

1 What Makes Gemstones Healing?

Gemstones.........contain life force. This life force is the divine energy that sustains, nourishes, and enlivens all living things

Guardian of Quartz
Gemisphere Luminary

Your Are a Being of Light

From your innermost essence to your physical body, you are made of and nourished by a continuous flow of life force. This life force is a current of light which springs from the source of life itself. When it flows freely, you experience joy, vitality, and vibrant health.

In the natural course of living, however, various blockages accumulate within this flow. These blockages create dark clouds within you. The obscure your radiance and give rise to disharmony, pain, and disease.

Gemstones Embody Life Force

Like us, the Earth is enlivened by life force. As the Earth was forming, life energy was infused into the planet's crystalline matrices. Thus, the Earth's gemstones come to embody and express the life force within the planet.

Gemstones Dissolve Blockages

Gemstones radiate their life force with great power. When used properly they can bring light into areas of darkness and neutralize blockages within your being. As these blockages dissolve, the light of the life force can once again shine through to enliven, nourish, and heal you. Each type of gemstone expresses a different frequency; therefore, it can address a different kind of blockage.

The Benefits of Gem Therapy

The proper stone can bestow fantastic benefits. There should also a be a strong meditation by the wearer of the result desired before beginning its use. Even in children, where the parents are the once devoting all the mental energy, we have seen dramatic improvements. The use of pearls with young children has been shown to be effective in helpingto calm hyperactivity. It seems to make them think with more clarity.

Gemstones Crystals: Gemstones Crystals- The Benefits of Gem Therapy

Gem Therapy for the Modern Age

The history of gemstone therapy dates back for thousand of year. It is known that the ancient Greeks, Egyptians, and Judaic cultures utilized gems for both healing and general enhancement of life, but it was the ancient Vedic culture of India that gave us the greatest inheritance of this knowledge. The metaphysical properties and how persons can increase their own well-being on the physical, emotional and even spiritual planes through the proper use of gemstones is a science delineated in the Vedic scriptures to a far greater degree than the texts of any other ancient culture.

Gemstones Crystals: Gem Therapy for the Modern Age

Vedic Gemstone Therapy

From time immemorial gemstones have been used by all coutures of the world. Their inherent beauty is second to no other material in the mineral kingdom. Today's science of gemology gives much information about the physical properties and chemical composition of gemstones, but gives no information of their "healing properties". They are extremely powerful tools to aid in balancing the physical, psychological and spiritual sides of life. This is necessary in order to keep oneself in proper order. The information I will give in this section in mainly from the Vedic viewpoint. This has been tried and tested for thousands of years and found to be accurate. The vedas have the greatest wealth of information on the metaphysical properties, as well as the physical properties, of gems and their correct application to enhance the lives of human beings more powerful than the wearer can bear. When choosing to war a gemstone, it is important to consider one's overall astrological chart and to understand the synergy between the various planets. It is best to have a qualified astrologer prescribe the gem. Sometimes more than one gem will be prescribed. Gems sometimes have more effect when worn on one day than on another. To receive a gemstone's effect, the gem must actually be worn; simply owning it is not enough.

Astrological Remedial Measures

Gems help to improve the effects planets have on us. To counter the malefic effects of a planet, one can also chant planetary mantras, platform sacrifices and worship, and give charity along with wearing the gem. These other activities also increase the gemstone's effect.

In general, gemstones should be worn to strengthen weak planets as calculated by the astrological chart. It is best to strengthen benefic planets when they are weak. Care should be taken when attempting to strengthen naturally malefic planets, such as Saturn and Ketu, and gems used for this purpose should definitely be prescribed by a qualified astrologer.

Gems are used in Eastern astrology to avert the negative influence of various planets or to increase their positive effects. The use of gems has been mentioned in the Vedic literature- the Brihat Samhita, Bhava Prakash, Ayurveda Prakash, Guruda Purana and the Rasa Ratna Samuchaya.

The gem therapy describe in this book is based on the Vedic (Indian) or sidereal system of astrology. Each sign of the zodiac is ruled by a planet, and each planet gives off a cosmic vibration and rules, or is related to, certain gemstones. The gems absorb or reflect the planet's vibration, or rays. Wearing the proper gem can increase a planet's positive effect on the wearer because the gem acts as a filter the allows only positive vibration to have influence.

Gems surround their wearer with an electromagnetic field. If a person is receiving a planet's negative rays, wearing the correct gemstone can counteract those bad effects and allow only the planet's positive effects to work on the person. Wearing a gemstone to counteract the malefic effects of a planet is like carrying an umbrella to avoid getting wet; the gemstone actually deflects a planet's negative rays.

It is important to note, however, that wearing the wrong gemstone can have a negative effect on the wearer. Wearing the wrong gems short-circuits the subtle body's energy fields. Thus physical or mental problems may result. Great care should be taking when using a gemstone of a naturally malefic planet to counter act its bad effects, as instead, it may increase the bad effects of the malefic planet.

To have maximum effect, the gemstone chosen should be of good quality. The better the gem's quality, the more powerful its effect. Do not wear cracked or chipped gems, as they can have a very detrimental effect. Thoroughly inspect gems for defects before purchasing them. The gem's size is also important. It is best that a precious stone be at least one carat; two or more carats are better. The maximum size for gems is determined by the type of gem. The less valuable the gem, the larger the stone should be to have the full effect.

2 How Does A Gem Function to Affect Human's Life

ll the planets have their individual colours, jewels and signs. However, the question is, how so the jewels and the gem work after all? What are the scientific explanations that tell us of the forces that make them work? It is necessary that we should discuss this, here.

We can take an example. The ultra-violet rays of the sun are considered very dangerous for a human life. If the fellow puts on a piece of ruby on person, the ruby would contain the ultra-violet rays and would not aloow them enter the human's body directly, save the Ruby-rays would be permitted in it. As a result of which the human's arteries and veins would function very well, his/her sensory feelings would be stronger, and he/she wuld gain the power of the Sun. By that, whichever rays of the sum that piece of ruby contains would invariably enter the human's body. That would affect his/her mind brian, thought -process, and the qualities of the rays would flourish in him/ her faster than without the Ruby. The similar results have been found in other planets.

What are the purpose of Gems

From times immemorial the gems and jewels were worn in person as an expression of make-up or ornamentation and as a display of wealth. The Ayurveda has in its tenets the subject such as the use of gems and jweles in human physiology and the relevant studies about it. For thousands of years Ayurvedacharyas have used the gems in forms of ashes, powders and for the chemical trials in treating human ailments (CF. Ratna Dweep by Dr. Gouri Shankar Kapur published in 1974 by Goyal to be highly auspicious. In almost all the religious functions, the Pancharatna was always in use. Thereafter, according to the tenets of Navagraha (a combination of nine planets, these gems were divided assigning the suitability of the time of influences of the planets. The gems such as, ruby, pear, coral, emerald, yellow sapphire, diamond, blue sapphire, zircon and the cat's eye or lapis lajuli were classified as Navaratna (as assortment of nine gems). However, it was Vrihatsamhita, in which the first lage list of the gems and jweels was given in Ratna Parikshadhyaya, Varahmihira had mentioned 22 gems in all, which are as under:

(1) Vajra (Diamond) (2) padmaraga (ruby) (3) vimalak (transparent) (4) market (emerald-green) (5) vaidurya (lapis lajuli) (6) sphatik (rock -crystal) (7) saugandhik (sulphur) (8) indraneel (blue sapphire) (9) rudhir (ruby) (10) rajmanhi (king of gems) (11) gomedak (12) pushparaga (Topaz), (13) Mukta (Pearl) (14) Samyak (15) shankh (coch-shell) (16) karketak (17) pulak (18) shashikanta (19) mahaneel (blue sapphire type) (20) jyotiras (21) brahmamanhi and (22) prabal (coral). Gems continue to be in use in India. Its popularity is spreading as always. In course of time, along with the precious stones too have become much in demand. As a result of which the gems and jewels dealers introduced a list of 84 gems which are socially accepted today. These are found in various colours, which can be worn according to the tenets of zodiac signs and their choice colours. Some call these stones as "Hakik" stones, which however, are not quite expensive.

3 Identification of Gems

A gem cannot always be identified by sight alone. It is therefore necessary to rely on measurement of the optical properties that can be determined without harming the stone in any way.

The gemologist uses an instrument called a refractometer to measure the characteristic property of the stone, known as refractive index, which is its relative ability to refract light. In addition, an instrument called the polariscope is employed to determine whether a gem is doubly or singly refracting. Emeralds, rubies, sapphires, amethysts, and synthetic rubies and sapphires are all doubly refracting, whereas diamonds, spinels, synthetic spinels, garnets, and glass are singly refracting. A special dark-field illuminator with a binocular microscope is employed for examining the interior of a gemstone to determine whether it is of natural or artificial origin, and to search for inclusions characteristic of a given gemstone.

These tests usually are sufficient to identify the rather limited number of materials used as gemstones; occasionally, however, other instruments are required, including a dichroscope, which measures the property called dichroism, or a spectroscope to determine the characteristic absorption spectra. Hardness, the test ordinarily associated with gem testing, is never used on cut stones by the gemologist.

Another physical test that can be given to an unknown stone is the determination of its specific gravity. For exact determinations various weighing devices are used, but rough approximations of the specific gravity of lighter stones can be made by means of a series of liquids of known specific gravity. If the stone will float in a liquid having a specific gravity of 4 and sink in a liquid with a specific gravity of 3, the specific gravity of the stone must lie between these limits and be approximately 3.5.

4 Gem Materials

The accompanying table lists precious and semiprecious gem minerals with the names commonly applied to them. See separate articles on many of the gems mentioned.

Artificial Gems

The term artificial gem is used to describe either an imitation of a natural gemstone or a synthetic gem that is chemically identical to naturally occurring gems.

Imitation Gems

Such a gem may be made of flint glass, often silvered on the back to increase the brilliance. Since World War II, colored plastics have replaced glass, especially in costume jewelry. Plastics are cheaper, more easily molded, and lighter in weight.

During the 19th century, artificial pearls were made by blowing hollow beads of glass and pouring into them a mixture of liquid ammonia and the white matter from the scales of fish such as the bleak, roach, or dace. A much better type of artificial pearl, the indestructible bead, was introduced shortly after 1900. The bead is made of solid glass with only a narrow hole for the thread. Pearl essence, consisting of the crushed scales of certain herring, is applied to the outside of the glass and covered with a transparent, colorless lacquer.

The most successful imitation of a diamond is strontium titanate, made by a flame-fusion technique. Its index of refraction is almost identical to that of a diamond, and it has a higher dispersion. Thus, it has the brilliance and greater fire than the diamond. It scratches easily, however. A harder material simulating the diamond is rutile, or titanium oxide.

5 Astrology And Gemstones Zodiac Signs And Stones

Astrology has allocated certain gemstones to each of the zodiac signs. In some cases, these coincide with the same stone as for the monthly birthstone charts, in others they differ. As with monthly birthstones, there are many differing opinions as to the appropriate gemstone for each sign. We will be adding further to this page later, with alternatives.

Zodiac	Gemstone	Symbol	From	To
Aquarius	Garnet	Water Carrier	January 20	February 18
Pisces	Amethyst	Fish	February 19	March 20
Aries	Bloodstone	Ram	March 21	April 20
Taurus	Sapphire	Bull	April 21	May 20
Gemini	Agate	Twins	May 21	June 20
Cancer	Eme rald	Crab	June 21	July 20
Leo	Onyx	Lion	July 21	August 21
Virgo	Cornelian	Virgin	August 22	September 22
Libra	Chrysolite	Scales	September 23	October 22
Scorpio	Beryl	Scorpion	October 23	November 22
Sagittarius	Topaz	Archer	November 23	December 20
Capricorn	Ruby	Goat	December 21	January 19

6 Birthstones

Over thousands of years, a tradition has developed, associating certain gemstones with times of the year.

It is likely that pagan beliefs associated the time of year of a person's birth with certain characteristics. Pagan cultures are ones in which the believers tend to be in tune with nature and the earth's cycles and seasons.

These pagan beliefs became incorporated into later religions including judaism and christianity. Astrology is also a link with these earlier beliefs.

With the passing of time and fashions, different gemstones have been ascribed to different months. It is thought that, originally, colour was the major attribute which determined a person's birthstone. During the eighteenth century, the connection between birthstones and particular months received a wave of popularity, and many different lists came into being.

Birthstones by Month

Month	Birthstone	Alternatives	Colour
January	Garnet		Dark Red
February	Amethyst		Purple
March	Aquamarine	Bloodstone	Pale Blue
April	Diamond	Rock Crystal	White
May	Emerald	Chrysoprase	Bright Green
June	Pearl	Moonstone	Cream
July	Ruby	Cornelian, Onyx	Red
August	Peridot	Sardonyx	Pale Green
September	Sapphire	Lapis Lazuli	Deep Blue
October	Opal	Tourmaline	Variegated
November	Topaz	Citrine	Yellow
December	Turquoise		Sky Blue

7 Choosing Your Personal Gem Stone

It is common today to have a personal stone. The personal stone may be associated with a zodiac sign or a birth month. It may be a gem stone that has been passed down in a family or even a favorite color. **Your personal stone is one with which you feel a deep connection.** Edgar Cayce said all gems have vibrations, but not all work the same on people. To have the best benefits from a stone there must be a deep feeling for the stone.

Methods you can use to discover your personal stone:

- • Planetary Gem Stones

In early Ayervedic and Tantric texts, certain gems were related to specific parts of the body. Nine stones are related to the planets and nodes of the moon. This method is often used by people who are having problems with a body part.

- • Zodiac Gem Stones

Another Eastern method of choosing your stone is by finding the stones that are linked to your sign of the zodiac. In this system, there are stones that should be avoided for each sign.

- • Birth Stones

In the West, as early as the fifth century AD, the twelve stones that adorned the breastplate of the Biblical Hebrew High Priest have been linked to the twelve zodiac signs, and later to the twelve months of the year.

• • Colored Gem Stones

Your instinctive reaction to various colors can help you to choose the right gemstone for you.

Use the color method to find stones that will help you over longer periods of time, or for a particular purpose. **Make sure you have a clear intention in mind when using this method.**

Gather a collection of paper, cloth or stones in these colors: Red, Pink, Brown, Orange, Yellow, Green, Blue, Purple, White, Black, Gray.

Place your selection of colors or colored stones before you.

Close your eyes and allow your breathing to settle.

Intend that you will be drawn to a stone or color when you open your eyes.

The color or stone upon which your gaze has fallen is your personal stone.

Choose from the colors of stones here if you used paper or cloth.

• • Gemstone Meanings

Some gemstones have qualities that seem to match your personality characteristics. These make useful personal stones. Another approach is to choose stones according to the qualities you want to develop in yourself. For example, if you have a hard time making decisions, you might choose a fluorite.

8 Gemstones

Gemstones, minerals that are treasured for their beauty and durability. A large number of minerals have been used as gems. Their value generally depends on four elements: the beauty of the stone itself; its rarity; its hardness and toughness; and the skill with which it has been cut and polished. Stones such as diamonds, rubies, and emeralds represent one of the greatest concentrations of money value.

Optical Properties

The beauty of gems depends to a large extent on their optical properties. The most important optical properties are the degree of refraction and color. Other properties include fire, the display of prismatic colors; dichroism, the ability of some gemstones to present two different colors when viewed in different directions; and transparency. Diamond is highly prized because of its fire and brilliancy, ruby and emerald because of the intensity and beauty of their colors, and star sapphire and star ruby because of the star effect, known as asterism, as well as for their color.

In certain gemstones, notably opals, brilliant areas of color can be seen within the stone; these areas change in hue and size as the stone is moved. This phenomenon, known as play of color, differs from fire and is caused by interference and reflection of the light by tiny irregularities and cracks inside the stone. Opals also exhibit milky or smoky reflections from within the gem. Gems that are fibrous in structure show irregular interior reflections similar to those seen on watered or moiré silk. This optical property, which is called chatoyancy, is exhibited by several gems, notably the tigereye and cat's-eye.

The appearance of a gem as seen by reflected light is another optical property of gemstones and is called luster. The luster of gems is characterized by the terms metallic, adamantine (like the luster of the diamond), vitreous (like the luster of glass), resinous, greasy, silky, pearly, or dull. Luster is particularly important in the identification of gemstones in their uncut state.

Gemmology or the scientific and ethnic study of gemstones is an integral part of applied Astrology under Remedial Measures and the use of precious gems & stones has been an age-old practice in India. Since ancient times Kings and Queens adore the ornaments along with Gems to enhance vitality, vigour, longevity, strength, fame, wealth and to ward of evil effects of malefic planets so as to bring happiness and prosperity to the native. Gemstones are minerals looked by way of their crystal structure and the physical properties viz. hardness, specific gravity, crystal shapes, optical properties, colour & luster. Scriptual evidences infer that the concept of precious gems & stones is as old as the Creation itself.

Sashankh Chakram Sakirit Kundalam, Sapeet Vastram Sarasi Runekshanam !!

Sahar Vaksh Sthal Kaustubhashriyam, Namami Vishnum Sirasa Chaturbhujam !!

(Above hymn narrates Lord Vishnu bears Kaustubha Mani- Gem on his chest, the most dear to Him, thus even before the whole Universe came into existence, the Gem Kaustubha existed along with Him)

Rig-Veda mentions the use of Ratnas (GEMS) i.e precious stones. Each gem stone has a specific light energy having rational behind curative power of the specific Gem under Remedial measures, thus scientifically they have the capacity to absorb all solar light & cosmic energy and emit a certain quality of light from amongst the seven basic colours of the visible spectrum of light, thus allowing a particular energy to flow through it which is being absorbed by the body. Among **Puranas**, Agnipurana and Garuda-Purana contains exhaustive description about precious gems & stones.

A scripture **VRIHAT SAMHITA** written by great scholar Varahmihir had devoted a whole chapter, Ratnadhyay giving comprehensive description of the Gemstones which is widely recognized among the gemologists.

Gems affects the subtle energy field, which emanates from every living thing, where our energetic and emotional habits, thought patterns, belief systems, and so on reside. The energy pattern of a gem directly affects one's emotional and mental energies, and over a period of time this promotes long-lasting changes. These remedial stones act in two ways; one is by its spectrum effects and other is by radioactive effects. When a ring is worn, Gem goes on continuously vibrating its power which is absorbed in the individual aura. The protective aura thus becomes powerful to resist any untoward vibrations coming from external sources.

<u>Gems are classified in to two types</u> : (a) **Hot** - Ruby, Red coral, Diamond and Cat's eye are Hot in nature. (b) **Cold** - Pearl, Topaz, Blue Sapphire and Gomedh are Cold in nature.

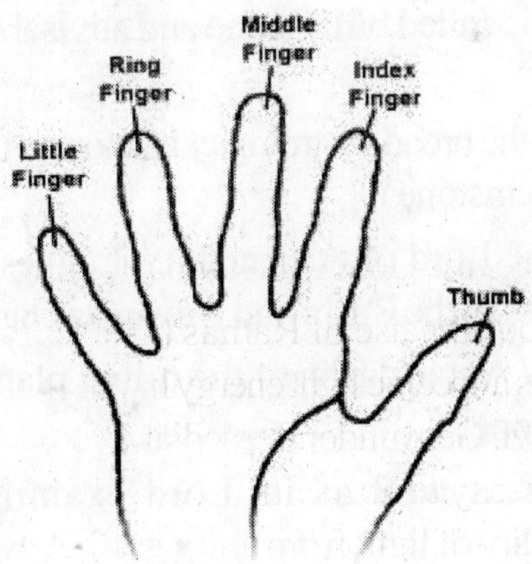

(**1**= Thumb, **2**= Index Finger, **3**= Middle Finger, **4**= Ring Finger, **5**= Little Finger)

FINGER	PLANET	BODY-PART	GEMS
Index (2)	Jupiter	Lungs,Stomach	Topaz, Yellow sapphire, Pearl
Middle (3)	Saturn	Liver, Intestine,Brain	Gomedh,Cats Eye, Blue Sapphire
Ring (4)	Sun	Stomach, Blood circulation	Ruby, Red Coral, Topaz
Little (5)	Mercury	Muscles, Nerves	Emerald

We select Gems to increase the beneficacy or reducing the malefic effects of the planets (Mars, Saturn, Rahu, Ketu, Sun, Waning Moon) posited in the birth horoscope of the native. **A** planet during his Maha-dasha or Antar-dasha is capable of producing malefic or benefic results pertaining to his natural characteristics (karakatwas) , the rashi and the bhavas he owns. Thus Gems are also recommended during the running period of Major/ Sub-periods apart from stengthening the Lagnesh in the natives horoscope. Gems are recommended on the basis of Ascendant (LAGANA), Lords of the Bhavas occupying Kendra or Trikona as well as YOGAKARAKS and during Major & Sub-periods of the malefic planets posited in the natives horoscope. Gem of Lagnesh is called birth-stone and advisable to wear for good health.

The following are the broad Astrological factors to be examined before prescribing the Gemstone :

1. Lagna and the Lord of Ascendant - Lagnesh checked for its auspiciousness in the Rashi and Navamsa chart.
2. Maha-dasha/ Antar-dasha of the ruling planet running in the native horoscope.
3. Moon Rashi as well as its Lord examined to check for auspiciousness.
4. The Janam Nakshatra including the Lord and its dispositor for auspiciousness.
5. Strength of all planets posited in Rashi chart.

6. Sign ownership of various planets i.e exaltation/ debilitation/ Friendly/ Enemy/ Neutral.
7. Chalit Kundli also to be seen for any planet changes its position house-wise.

LAGAN	MALEFICS	BENEFICS	YOGAKARAKS	GEMSRECOMMENDED
Mesha	Saturn, Mercury, Venus	Jupiter, Sun	——	Moonga
Vrishabha	Jupiter, Venus, Moon	Saturn,Sun	**Saturn**	Heera
Mithuna	Mars, Jupiter, Sun	Venus	——	Panna
Karkata	Venus, Mercury	Mars,Jupiter	**Mars**	Moti
Simha	Mercury,Venus	Mars	——	Manik
Kanya	Mars, Jupiter,Moon	Venus	**Venus,Mercury**	Panna
Thula	Jupiter, Sun, Mars	Saturn, Mercury	**Moon, Mercury**	Heera
Vrischika	Mercury, Mars,Venus	Moon	**Sun, Moon**	Moonga
Dhanu	Venus	Mars,Sun	**Sun, Mercury**	Pukhraj
Makara	Mars, Jupiter, Moon	Venus,Mercury	**Venus**	Neelam
Kumbha	Jupiter, Moon, Mars	Venus	**Mars**	Neelam
Meena	Saturn, Venus, Sun, Mercury	Mars,Moon	**Mars, Jupiter**	Pukhraj

FUNCTIONAL SIGNIFICANCE :

Ruby (Manik) - Sun, our soul

Ruby is said to give name, fame, virtue, vigor, warmth and commanding power to its user. It also enhances the status of a person as well as nobility, dignity, power, leadership, and confidence. The native will be well-read, pious, strong, compassionate, and untroubled. It is red in color and medically helps to cure peptic ulcer, fever, rheumatism, gout. Ruby should be used in Gold. Semi Precious substitute stone : Red Garnet. (**Mantra - "Om ghrinih suraya namah "**)

Pearl (Moti) - Moon, our mind

Pearl is used to remove the evil effects of moon and it strengthens the mind and enhances the good sleep and cures insomnia.. One will be wealthy, sensitive, good habits, stable, healthy, industrious and respected. It is white in colour and strengthens memory, cures uterine disorders, heart trouble and eye diseases, hysteria and pleurisy etc. It also increases sexual strength and makes the conjugal life happy, removes melancholy and increases fortune. Semi-Precious substitute stone : Moon stone, Opal. (**Mantra - "Om som somaaya namah"**)

Red Coral (Moonga)- Mars, our efforts & protection

Red Coral instills courage and boldness in its user. It also helps in curing blood related diseases. This is normally red in color. Coral ensures positive energy, strength, courage, passion, aggression, material happiness & recovery from diseases indicated by Mars such as fever, cough etc. One will be active, have great energy, be learned, well-known and regal.

Semi-Precious substitute stone : Carnelian. (**Mantra - "Om ang angarkaaya namah"**)

Emerald (Panna) - Mercury, our communication skills

It increases intelligence and brain power. It improves faculties related to brain such as memory, communication, intuition, the intellect ability to learn, rationality, wit, skillfulness, and dexterity. One will be educated, happy, fortunate, and highly respected. It is advised that newly wed couples should avoid wearing this as it impairs conjugal happiness due to reduction in sexual desires. Semi-Precious substitute stone : Peridot. (**Mantra - "Om bum budhaaya namah"**)

Yellow Sapphire (Pukhraj) / Topaz - Jupiter, our spiritual teacher

Yellow sapphire gemstones are very useful in astrology and vedic properties. It has many healing powers and is very important in star signs. It is said that this gem enhances financial status, gives wealth, good health, fame, name, honour, humanitarianism, spiritualism, optimism, faith and good judgment. One will be powerful, respected, and a leader of men, although susceptible to anger. **Topaz** is one of the most widely used gems to help achieve better financial status. It is also believed that if there are obstructions in finding a suitable match for a girl, she gets married by wearing Topaz. This is normally yellow in color. It improves vision, gives life security, protects one from poverty, removes adversity, misfortune and melancholy. Semi-Precious substitute stone : Golden Topaz. (**Mantra - "Om vrim brihaspataye namah"**)

Diamond (Heera) – Venus , luxuries & vehicles

Diamond denotes a luxurious life & supposed to enhance the name, fame, attractiveness, grace, elegance, longevity and artistic quality to the native. It also enhances sexual power & medically cures diabetes, diseases of urine and venereal diseases, skin and uterine diseases.. One will be refined, humanitarian, and possess many positive qualities. Semi-Precious substitute stone : Tourmaline , Rock crystal. (**Mantra -"Om shum shukraaye namah"**)

Blue Sapphire (Neelam) - Saturn, our duties & salvation

Blue Sapphire removes evil effects of Saturn and has the magical power to elevate its user to a higher status from all sides.. One will be long-lived, charitable, proficient, disciplined, responsible, realistic , durabable, humble and an affectionate mate. It could give you everything you could desire such as health, wealth, longevity, happiness. It also restores lost wealth and property & improves fertility in a barren women. However there is a caution as sometimes this stone may react adversely thus suggested that Blue Sapphire should be tested for one week before final wearing . Semi-Precious substitute stone : Turquoise, Lapis Lazuli. (**Mantra -"Om sham shanayisharaaye namah"**)

Gomed (Gomedh) - Rahu which represents our present karma

This Gem is for Shadow planet Rahu. The Shadow planet Rahu is supposed to be responsible for all sorts of delays or very late fulfillment of ambitions. Gomed can help in achieving speedy success in less time than expected.. One will be exotic, wealthy, fortunate & gives originality, inspiration, insight, and uniqueness to the native. Gomed is normally reddish-chocolate in color. It cures diseases caused by affliction of Rahu and Saturn. It also increases appetite, vitality, confers good health, wealth, happiness and all sound prosperity. Semi-Precious substitute stone : Zircon, Amber. (**Mantra - "Om ram'g rahve namah"**)

Cat's Eye (Lahasuniya) - Ketu, which represents our past karma

Cat's eye is useful for eradicating evil influences of Ketu and diseases given by Mars. This protects the native from hidden enemies, mysterious dangers and diseases.. One will be wealthy, protected from evil and imparts spiritualism, intuition, universality, subtleness and sensitivity This is normally milky in color. For businessmen, it is a miraculous result giving stone as bestows wealth by secret means like horse racing, gambling, stock exchange market and speculations. Semi-Precious substitute stone : Alexandrite

(**Mantra -"Om kem ketve namah"**)

The Gem should touch the body for the cure and to be worn on specified Finger/ Metal & specific days of Shukla Paksha on a suitable

Muhurata after worshipping and reciting the Mantra of that planet. The Gems of Lords of Trik -Bhavas (6th/8th/12th Houses) not to be worn due to to evil houses rather prophylactic and charity measures are the best suited.

Planets	Primary Gems	Secondary	Colour	Metal	Finger	Auspicious Day	Wght (Rattis)
Sun	Manik	Surya kanti	Dark red	Gold	Ring	Sunday	3/5/7
Moon	Moti	Safade Akeekh	White	Silver	Ring	Monday	4/6/8
Mars	Moonga	Sindoori Akeekh	Red	Copper	/ Little Ring	Tuesday	6-10
Mercury	Panna	Jabarajed / Peridote	Green	Gold /Bronze	Little	Wednesday	5/7/9
Jupiter	Pukhraj	Sunehle	Yellow	Gold	Index	Thursday	7/9/12
Venus	Heera	Zirokne/ White coral	White	Gold	Little	Friday	¼, ¾ ½
Saturn	Neelam	Amethyste / Laajvarti	Black	Steel / Iron	Middle	Saturday	14/7/10
Rahu	Gomedh	Taamerha /Agateh / Kala Akeekh	Blue	Lead /Panchdhatu	Middle	Saturday evening	4/5/7
Ketu	Lahsuniya	Lapuz Lazuli / Kala Akeek	Stray	Panchdhatu	Middle /Ring	Tuesday morning	4/5/7/9

n Modern times Gems and Jewellery has become consumerist :osmetic & vanity business where the native is unaware about the :onflict as well as the cosmic power of the Gems. Thus it is equally ignificant area for a qualified Astrologer to prescribe combination of

Gems at different points of time to derive maximum benefits & avoid conflict of various Gemstones by judging the planetary positions in the horoscope of the native.

PLANET	IMCOMPATIBILITY	CONFLICTING
Sun	Venus,Saturn,Rahu,Ketu	RUBY with diamond, blue sapphire, cats eye
Moon	Rahu, ketu	PEARL with hessonite & cats eye
Mars	Mercury, Saturn	RED CORAL with emerald, blue sapphire
Mercury	Moon	EMERALD with pearl
Jupiter	Mercury, Venus	YELLOW SAPPHIRE with emerald, diamond
Venus	Sun, Moon	DIAMOND with ruby, pearl
Saturn	Sun, Moon, Mars	BLUE SAPPHIRE with ruby, pearl, red coral
Rahu	Sun, Moon	HESSONITE with ruby, pearl
Ketu	Sun, Moon	CATS EYE with ruby, pearl

Conclusion: The Rig-Veda describes the use of Gems to capture the visible spectrum in the rays of the Sun. Astrological Gem Stone Therapy is prescribed on the bases of long-term known as Fortune Stones by judging the inherent placement of planets in the horoscope or the short-term (temporary periods) for providing relief during Mahadasha/ Antardasha / Gochar of malefic planets in the natives horoscope. Thus the Gems act according to the placement of benefic (favourable- Anukul Graha) and malefic planets (unfavourable - Pratikul Graha).

9 Gems And Their General Characteristics

RUBY or MANAK: Ruby or manak is a precious gemstone ruled by rajasik planet sun. It mainly emits red. infrared cosmic rays. Wearer of Ruby is bestowed with good health, position, prestige and favours from govt. officials & rulers. Persons having sun as benefic or yogakark should wear Ruby. Ruby is the stone of the SUn. and wearing of Ruby will protect the native from harmful effects of Sun's afflictions. Ruby is in red color, yellow color, violet mixed red color and in rose color. Ruby will protect one from ill health and grant success in administrative fields, freedom from enemies, debts and diseases. It ensures a long life and promotes independence.

General Characteristic of Ruby

1. Precious Ruby offers high honour & position.
2. Recommended for those in position of authority, those aspiring to become high dignitaries.
3. Highly suggested for rulers, politician dealing with affairs of nation.
4. It's a hot gem and ladies should avoid it specially in summer.
5. It enhances super ego & dominating characters.

PEARL or MOTI - Pearl or moti is ruled by moon. the cool calming planet of Hindu astrology. It is aggregate of sea salts, formed by shellfish under the int1uence of an irritating agent. Pearl coming from 'Basra are of pure quality and highly recommended for reducing mental agitations marital discords. Per.; on having moon as yogakarak or benefic should always use pearl. Pearl is the stone of the Moon and wearing of Pearl will protect the native from harmful effects of Moon afflictions. Pearls are available in many colors, but of all the colors, white and red coloured pearls are the best. Round pearls are superior. Flat type pearls should never be worn. Wearing of pearl helps the native get freedom from mental disturbances, happiness from mother, success in educational fields and ensures good health, long life and improves finances. It cures mental disorders, gastric disorders, asthma, breathing troubles and lung disorders.

General characteristics of Pearl

1 Pearl in silver can mitigate several million tensions.

2. Persons those have moveable mind and can't take decisions if wear pearl and in addition also recite Gayatri mantra* for 30 days, will obviously find soothing effect on mind and will be able to take quick decisions.

3. It enhances memory and concentration. These be used by scholars or students those want to make mark in the class or want to appear in competitive exams.

   (Students with poor concentration and failures should use green tourmaline + Emerald along with pearl.)

4. It enhances personal charm and recommended for fair sex.

5. It enhance optimism in love affairs, and power of understanding.

6. Real pearl string round the neck ofladies will preserve their chasity

7. It keeps the wearer away from ill reputed persons or unhealthy practices.

8. A good quality pearl minimum of 5.25 ratti acts as protective shield in stromy weather.

9. Wearer also gets self-confidence & enhance mental faculties.

10. Good for those engaged in humanitarian activities like hospital, etc.

RED CORAL or MOONGA - Moonga Red coral is gem bestowed with benefic influences of MARS. It provides vitality, vigour & stamina. Thc encrgy source red coral in highly recommended for the men in uniform. In usual practice it's oftcn recommended for gencral good luck and to enhance determination or will power. Person those are ruled by MARS or those have MARS as yogakarak should always wear 'Moonga'. Red coral is ruled by Mars is generally of red color. It may even be of orange red color. Red coral will bestow good health, longevity, courage, name, fame and happiness. The native would be blessed with children, intelligence, good fortune and success in professional life. It would also grant land and property, domestic harmony and gain of wealth. It cures all kinds of mental diseases, physical diseases and difficulties. It saves one from natural calamities like thunder, floods and fires. Its use also helps in removing impediments that could be delaying one's marriage. Woman with history of aboltion should wear this for successful delivery.

General characteristic of Moonga

1. Highly recommended for newly wedded couples.
2. Senior executives, soldiers, Army personnel, police men all may use it to enhance general luck.
3. To enhance stamina, vitality & energy in deblitiating diseases.
4. Recommended for dentists & surgeons.
5. Provide courage to those involved in litigation & propeliy disputes to over come obstacles.

6. Mangliks, those are not getting married should wear Moonga.
7 Protects the wearer from tropical fever, accidents and unexpected happenings.

EMERALD or PANNA- Mercury the ruler of intelligence rules Emerald or Panna. It's green coloured soft gem never comes without intermingling fibres within and it's also the identification mark of true or fake gem. It's notable that when mercury in Virgo, It may bring native to the top of academic or literary fields unless badly aspected. Emerald is ruled by Mercury. This is a beautiful velvety green colored stone. The Emerald with a deep velvet green to grass green color, radiant, smooth, transparent and with bright rays is the best and most auspicious Gem. Emerald helps in acquiring wealth and the native would be blessed with children, intelligence, good health, wealth, longevity, l,!nds and prosperity, domestic happiness and an obstruction free life. It brings advancement in profession, name, fame and honour. It cures eye diseases, controls B.P. and nervous disorders and turns enemies into friends.

General characteristic of Emerald

1. Highly effective for perfect control are nervous system. Defects of memory concentration, stammering etc. essentially require Emerald.
2. Combust or deb. Mercury often gives lung problems (Asthma, bronchites) and may give rise to academic downfall, here good quality emerald creates wonders.
3. Businessmen, writers, publishers, authors may liberally use emerald.
4. It's good for those are lazy or those need control over tongue or engaged in communication.

5. It should not be worn by newly married couples, as it decreases sexual appetite and performance. NB - If essential, must worn with Red Coral.

PUKHRAJ - "Pukhraj" or "Pushprag" / yellow sapphire, is used for getting the benevolent blessings of .Jupiter. It is an expensive stone and denotes righteousness, piety and truthfulness. It is often recommended for economic prosperity. Persons who are ruled by .Jupiter or those have Jupiter as beneifc or yogakaraka, must weal' a Pukhraj. It is the Stone ohhe .Jupiter and wearing ohhis gem protects the native from harmful effects of .Jupiter's aft1ictions. It is available in light yellow or golden color. It should be heavy, transparent and glittering. Yellow Sapphire will make one intellectual, charitable, religious and respectable towards elders. It ensures wealth, name and fame. It will bless the native with good childeren. It also acts as a protective charm. Those who find obstruction in the progress of their educational field, or those who suffer losses from property matters should wear Yellow Sapphire for removal ohheir difficulties

General characteristics of Pukhraj

1. Its beneficial for political and intellectual success.
2. Transforms the native into a highly pious and religious person. Protects the wearer from evil thoughts.
3. Protects the native from damages during long voyages.
4. Blesses one with child and facilitates marriage of a girl.
5. Promotes services matters, increments of professional interest.

DIAMOND - Diamond the hardest substance on earih is often preferred by ladies for beauty, status and jewellery purpose. However astrologically diamond is not much preferred gem unless specified.

Diamond I'lded by Venus often benefit the wearer pretty fast if Venus is well placed in the chali. The two essentials of good quality are colour & clearity. Diamond is ruled by Venus. Diamonds are white, blue, red and black colored. It ensures longevity and advancement in life. It can bless the native with children, happiness, intelligence, name, fame and good fOitune. It ensures abundant wealth and success in all ventures. It cures the diseases of kidney and reproductive organs. It drives away evil spirits and bad effects of evil eyes. It ensures happy married life, possession of jewellery and ornaments, rich dress, conveyances, comfortable house and bilth of good children.

General characteristics of Diamond

1. Facilitates marital happiness for ladies.
2. Enhance talents and success is art, drawing, theatre, and movies.
3. Enhance interest in sexual acts and also increase performance.
4. Provides success in couris, litigation etc.
5. Increases longevity & general financial prosperity.
6. It also act as nutritious pacifier for several dosha and may cure many ailments.
7. Effective in facial paralysis, pneumonia, bronchitis, diabetes, gynecological disorders. 8 Enhance sincerity in love and devotion towards spouse.

BLUE SAPPHIRE (NEELAM) - Due to unstable nature of Neelam bringing only extremities, It gives very beneficial results once suited but may destroy the whole life if unsuitable. It is not uncommon to observe malefic effects bring by Neelam even though it appears suitable in the nativity. That is why it's always taken on trial first and if it doesn't show any harm during the trial period it may be got set in the ring.

During trial it may manifest it's harm by a continuous new and acute headache, minor accidents, pain in abdomen, bad news, delays in almost all ventures. Nee]am kept under the pillow for atleast three nights regularly the quality of dreams are sufficient to tell about suitability of gem. Minimum trial over body should be of ten days. Neelam is ruled by Saturn, the planets of hardships and struggle thus it's obvious that it will be suitable to very few natives, but once suited it's one of the greatest blessings. This is ruled by the planet Satul'Jl. Blue Sapphire is availab]e in dark, ordinary or light blue colors. B]ue Sapphire is believed to give very beneficial results. But in case it proves unsuitable, it could destroy the life of the native. This Gem should be WOI'Jl only after a trial. By wearing Blue Sapphire one gets good servants. The native will always enjoy happiness, prosperity, name and fame, advancement in profession and favours from government. It bestows good health and success in all ventures. The native will get land, building and properties. It also ensures success in politics. One could become either a King or a great scholar by wearing Blue Sapphire.

General characteristics of Neelam

1. It can cause sudden upturn in business and change the life pattern for good.
2. Protects wearers from unexpected happenings & natural calamity.
3. It may give rapid & immense financial gain & rajayoga
4. Best for depressive psychosis frustration, alcoholism.
5. Khooni Neelam (Red & Blue Neelam) is very useful when sat is aspected or conjuncted by MARS or Rahu in natal charts. It's "shrapit" (curse) condition and khooni Neelam provides financial & marital prosperity.
6. Highly useful when tuberculosis is chronic.

NB - Other substitute therapy is Red coral for chronic TB 7. Infetiility problems, use it along with green tourmaline.

GOMEDHA AND CAT'S EYE - Rahu & ketu are two shadowy planets, those are actually not planets but the nodes. The ascending nods or caput or Dragon's head is Rahu, while the descending nodes ,or cauda or Dragon's tail is Ketll. In Indian Astrology Rahu is taken as second Saturn and ketu is taken as second MARS. In-addition they also behave like the planets, which rule the sign where they are deposited. Rahu rules Gomedha and ketll rules cat's eye. Gomeda is the Gem Stone of Rahu. It's color varies from red, smoky to honey color. Use of Gomeda will bestow good health, victory over enemies and bring wealth and prosperity to its owner. It cures diseases, gives knowledge and intelligence. It promotes good education and ensures improvement in the profession. Native's business will flourish. The adverse effects caused by evil also vanish. One gets quite active by wearing Gomeda and gets promotion in the service. It can give unexpected wealth to its wearer. It bestows a very happy life, and the enmity of relatives disappears. Evil spirits go away. It ensures sound sleep and gives peace of mind. Cat's Eye is Gem Stone of Ketll. This is yellowish or blackish in color. Inside there is a shining band which moves when the stone is turned. This is a quick action Gem and restores lost wealth. Povetiy and diseases vanish. It ensures victory over enemies and protection from enemies. By wearing a Cat's eye one is be attracted by others. It grants philosophical disposition and activity ofthe mind. The native gets name, fame and wealth. He becomes calm and his anger disappears. He receives the help of relatives and friends. Enemies may bow to him. It works successfully in getting back the loan money too. It ensures the welfare of children. Childless person lllay be blessed with children. It protects from accidents, pimples and skin diseases. It ensures quick marriage.

General characteristics of Gomedha (Hessonite)

1. It colours like cow's urine.
2. Helps the wearers with regard to professional advancement, finances, and health.
3. Highly recommended where Rahu is in 10th house or / and person involved in politics.
4. These are involved in legal professions may also wear Gomedha.
5. Very useful for undiagnosed diseases, where its use facilitates fast diagnosis.
6. It protects wearer from unforeseen calamities & diseases during voyages.

General Characteristics of Cat's eye

1. It resembles with "Nimbori" (Neems fruit) with a silver streak. However it comes in varigiated colours.
2. It is effective when ketu's placing is not good in the chart and Ketu is causing ill reputation and increased rivalries.
3. Those are prone to scandals & loss of reputation may use it.
4. It relives fear of hardships and increases determination.
5. It works well when ketu is placed in 6,8,12 house from Venus.

Planet	Sign Ruled	Primary Gem	Secondary Gem	3rd Choice	4th Choice
Sun	Leo	Ruby	Red Spinel	Rhodolite	Almandite
Moon	Cancer	Natural Pearl	Tissue Nucleated Pearl	South Sea Pearl	Moonstone
Mars	Aries, Scorpio	Red Coral	*	*	Carnellion
Mercury	Gemini, Virgo	Emerald	Green Tourmaline	Peridot	*
Jupiter	Sagittarius Pisces	Yellow Sapphire	Yellow Topaz	Yellow Beryl	Citrine
Venus	Taurus,	Diamond Libra	White	Danburite Sapphire	White Topaz
Saturn	Capricorn, Aquarius	Blue Sapphire	Tanzanite	Amethyst	*
Rahu	*	Hessonite	Orange Zircon	Spessartite	*
Ketu	*	Chrysoberyl	*	*	*

Planet	Gem of Planet	Hindi Name	Nature of Gem	Color of
Gem.	Sun	Ruby	Manak	Hot Orange
Moon	Pearl	Moti	Cold	White
Mars	Coral	Moonga	Hot	Red
Mercury	Emerald	Panna	Hot	Green
Jupiter	Yellow Sapphire	Pukhraj	Cold	Yellow
Venus	Diamond	Hira	Hot	Transparent
Saturn	Blue Sapphire	Neelam	Too Cold	Blue
Rahu	Hessonite	Gomed	Hot	Ultra Voilet
Ketu	Cat's Eye	Lahsaniya	Too Cold	Indefinable

Gemstones and 12 Ascendants

Sign:	Favorable Colors:	Unfavorable Colors:	Favorable Gems:	Unfavorable Gems:
Aries:	Pink, orange, white, red, yellow, royal blue, navy blue, bright brown, bright black, and variegated.	Green, grey, and faded colors.	Ruby, pearl, red coral, yellow sapphire, diamond, and blue sapphire.	Emerald, hessonite, and cat's eye.
Taurus:	Pink, orange, white, green, navy blue, bright brown, bright black.	Grey, dull brown, faded colors, yellow, royal blue, red, variegated colors.	Ruby, pearl, emerald, blue sapphire.	Red coral, yellow sapphire, diamond, hessonite, cat's eye.
Gemini:	Pink, orange, white, red, green, yellow, royal blue, variegated colors, navy blue, bright brown, bright black.	Steel grey, dull brown, faded colors.	Ruby, pearl, red coral, emerald, yellow sapphire, diamond,, blue sapphire.	Hessonite, cat's eye.
Cancer:	Pink, orange, white, red, green, royal blue, variegated.	Grey, dull brown, faded colors, navy blue, bright brown, bright black, yellow.	Ruby, pearl, red coral, emerald, and diamond.	Yellow sapphire, blue sapphire, hessonite, cat's eye.
Leo:	Pink, orange, red, green, yellow, royal blue, variegated colors, navy blue, bright brown, bright black.	White, grey, dull brown, faded colors.	Ruby, red coral, emerald, yellow sapphire, diamond, blue sapphire.	Pearl, hessonite, cat's eye.
Virgo:	White, green, yellow, royal blue, variegated.	Orange, bright black, bright brown, red, pink, grey, dull brown, navy blue, faded colors.	Pearl, emerald, yellow sapphire, diamond.	Red coral, ruby, blue sapphire, hessonite, cat's eye.
Libra:	Pink, orange, white, red, yellow, royal blue, variegated, navy blue, bright brown, bright black.	Green, smoke grey, steel grey, dull brown, faded colors.	Ruby, pearl, red coral, yellow sapphire, diamond, blue sapphire.	Emerald, hessonite, cat's eye.
Scorpio:	Pink, orange, white, green, yellow, navy blue, bright brown, bright black.	Red, royal blue, steel grey, dull brown, variegated, faded colors.	Ruby, pearl, emerald, yellow sapphire, blue sapphire.	Red coral, diamond, hessonite, cat's eye.
Sagittarius:	Pink, orange, red, green, yellow, royal blue, variegated, navy blue, bright brown, bright black.	White, steel grey, dull brown.	Ruby, red coral, emerald, yellow sapphire, diamond, blue sapphire.	Pearl, hessonite, cat's eye.
Capricorn:	Bright black, white, bright brown, all shades of blue, green, red, and variegated.	Steel grey, dull smoke grey, orange, pink, yellow, faded colors.	Blue sapphire, red coral, pearl, emerald, diamond.	Ruby, yellow sapphire, hessonite, cat's eye.
Aquarius:	Bright black, bright brown, red, orange, pink, yellow, variegated, all shades of blue.	White, grey, green, dull brown, faded colors.	Blue sapphire, red coral, ruby, diamond, yellow sapphire.	Pearl, emerald, hessonite, cat's eye.
Pisces:	White, red, green, yellow.	Grey, dull brown, faded colors, pink, orange, royal blue, variegated, navy blue, bright brown, bright black.	Pearl, red coral, emerald, yellow sapphire.	Ruby, diamond, blue sapphire, hessonite, cat's eye.

10 Emerald Gemstone

Gemological Properties Emerald

Chemical Composition	Be3A12Si603+Cr
Colour	From light yellowish green to dark bluish green and everything in between.
Hardness	7.5-8
Destiny	2.68-2.78
Refractive Index	1.577-1.593
Briefringence	0.005-0.009

Occurence

The finest emeralds are from Colombia at Chivor, Muzo, Gachala and Coscuez mines. Other fine emeralds come from Brazil, Zambia, Pakistan, Russia, Tanzania (Lake Manyara). Colombian emeralds from Muzo and Coscuez can be distinguished in a general way because Muzo material is blue- green, whereas that from Coscuez is yellowish green.

Astrological Healing Properties Emeral PANNA)

Planet	Mercury
Cosmic Colour	Green
Day	Wednesday
Time	Sunrise
Number	5
Chakra	1st, Sahasrana
Mercury Mantra	Aum bum bhudaya namah repeated 9 times at the time of wearing a Mercury talisman.
Element	Earth
Sign	Gemini & Virgo

Description: A member of the Beryl family which varies in colour from light to deep green.

Enhances: memory, courage, spiritual insight, psychic abilities, honesty, balance physical/ emotional/ mental bodies, meditation, self expression, tranquility.

Aids the maintenance or treatment of: suffering in spinal region (use with diamonds), fertility, depression, midchest problems, immune system, eye ailments, high blood pressure.

Special Features: The emerald should not be worn constantly but only when needed. **Where to wear:** Over the heart, ring finger or light arm.

Chakra: heart

Zodiac: Cancer / Scorpio / Taurus

Birthstone: May

Dream: Signifies a lot to look forward to

Care: Can be washed under luke warm water with a drop of detergent and water softener- rinse well in clear water as the soapy film can detract from the stone lustre. Can split if cleaned in ultrasonic cleaner.

A sophisticated gemstone

Whilst its good hardness protects the emerald to a large extent from scratches, its brittleness and its many fissures can make cutting, setting and cleaning rather difficult. Even for a skilled gem cutter, cutting emeralds presents a special challenge, firstly because of the high value of the raw crystals, and secondly because of the frequent inclusions.

However, this does not detract from the cutters' love of this unique gem. Indeed, they have developed a special cut just for this gem: the emerald cut. The clear design of this rectangular or square cut with its bevelled corners brings out the beauty of this valuable gemstone to the full, at the same time protecting it from mechanical strain. Emeralds are also cut in many other, mainly classical shapes, but if the raw material contains a large number of inclusions, it may often be cut into a gently rounded cabochon, or into one of the emerald beads which are so popular in India.

Today, many emeralds are enhanced with colourless oils or resins. This is a general trade practice, but it does have the consequence that these green treasures react very sensitively to inappropriate treatment. For example, they cannot be cleaned in an ultrasonic bath. The substances that may have been used by the cutter during his work, or applied subsequently, seal the fine pores in the surface of the gem. Removing them will end up giving the stone a matt appearance. For this reason, emerald rings should always be taken off before the wearer puts his or her hands in water containing cleansing agent.

Healing properties of Emerald

Emerald can help heal the physical heart as well as love. Emerald will help backaches when worn on the index finger of the left hand. A healer can use the ring while the patient lies on his stomach. The healer would hold the ring about 2 inches above the backbone and slowly make small circles up and down the spine. The power of the Emerald is highest at the full moon.Some cultures thought the emerald would heal any disease of the eye. The emerald would be placed in a container of water overnight and the water would be poured on the eyes the next day.Emerald is a stone of great harmony, wisdom and love. Giving your lover an Emerald will bring the lover closer if the giver's motives are pure love. The Emerald can be a bridge between 2 people. The Emerald vibrates with love.

11 Pearl

Chemical Composition	CACO3(aragonite)-about 82-86% conchiolin-about10-14%;Water2%
Colour	The colour of a pear is the result of a body colour and an overtone colour (known as orient) present (due to surface effects) as a lustrous sheen. White, light cream, light rose, light yellow, blue and green overtones on a white body, black and coloured pearls.
Hardness	2.5-4.5
Density	2.6-2.78, conch pearl, 2.85; cultured pearls, 2.72-2.78, i.e. heavier than most natural pearls, but this is not a diagnostic fact.
Occurence	Saltwater pearls are the most important on the market place. These come principally from the Persian gulf (coasts of Iran, Oman, Saudi Arabia and Bahrain State), Gulf of Manaar (an arm of the Indian Ocean between India and Ceylon), Australia, South Seas, Japan, Venezuela. Freshwater pearls come from rivers throughout the world.

Planet	Moon
Cosmic Colour	Orange
Number	2
Chakra	10th, Svadtistana
Moon Mantra	" Aum Som Somaya Namah" repeated 1 time at the time of wearing a moon talisman. "Born from the wind from the air, from the lightning, from the light, born from the gold, may the pearl protect us from any fear"
Sign	Cancer
Time	Evening
Day	Monday
Element	Water
Sign of a well placed Venus	Signs of an afflicted Moon "Pearl recommended"
	The native will have good affluence, good fortune, recognition and fame. Emotions under control. Good Memory. Balanced emotional life. Success, happiness and comfort able life can be rather difficult to achieve. Sicknesses during child hood. Fluctuations, moodiness, instability. Indecisions, lack of mental balance. Desire to lie and spread false rumors. Suffering from anxiety.
Sanskrit Names	Mukta, Pearl, Sasi-ratna, Gem of the moon, Taraka, Falling star, Jiva-ratna, Gem of the intellect.

12 Red Coral (Lal Moonga)

Planet	Mars
Cosmic Color	Yellow
Number	9
Chakra	7th, Muladhara
Red Coral Mantra	"Aum ang angarakaya namah" repeated 19 times at the time of wearing a Mars talisman.
Signs of a wellplaced Mars	Great energy and motivation. Courage, charisma, leadership. Physical strength, forcefulness. Ambition. Rapid advancement and success. Acquiring properties. Mechanical and technical jobs.
Signs of an afflicted Mars	" Red coral recommended" Aggressiveness, temper, argumen fights, accidents, violence, rebel lions, fire. Constant surgical operations. War or family arguments.
Prevention of the follwoing diesases	Eruptions of the face and body cuts burns, bruises General diseases of the blood, muscular system, bone marrow.
Element	Earth
Sign	Aries & Scorpio
Sanskrit Names	Munga, red coral, Bhauma-ratna, Gem of Mars, Vidruma, The coral tree, Abdhijantu, Being of the ocean.

13 White Coral

Coral is a precious gem of bright red colour and it comes in lighter shades too. Corals flourish at the hollow of the seas. An opaque gemstone is most effective for female or male for radiating powerful emotions through absorption or red rediation from visible light spectrum. Through the use of Coral, in gold several diseases can be warded off, particularly tropicla fevers, chicken pox, jaundice, fistula, impotency and ailments pertaining to blood, effective in healing ailments like anaemia general inflamations, cough and cold, bronchitis, pneumonia etc.

It helps to improve marital life, children suffering from malnutrition or inadequate/ slow development may also improve. Abortion or miscarriage or other prenatal compications can be prevented, provided the gem is used under expert guidence after three months of pregnancy. Police personal or defence officials would also be highly benefitted and protected from untoward happening and dangers. At times, nightmares or threats from inferior spirits or witchcrafts can be warded off. It also protects the from lightening and thunder abd traffic accidents. Some use its powder for improving disgestive system. Usually, those with birth number 9 would find instant results, as it would provide them with extra energies, financial stability, reduction of tensions, easing of litigation, vigour and issues, however entangeled and complicated those may be. It will give strengthen and willingness to dmeet challenges and critical situations. Some occultists have commended about its beneficial effect in curring natives from mysterious diseases and protecting them from untoward happenings as also from sudden and unexpected developments. It is good for those sufffering from diabetes. Hindu ladies can use these gems probably engraved with an image of Hanumanji. It should be preferable worn on Tuesdays within one hour of the sunrise.

Healing properties of coral

Coral symbolizes life and blood force energy. Dark red coral is used for heating and stimulating the bloodstream. Pink shades restore harmony to the heart. It is used as an aid to depression, lethargy or deficient nutrition.

Sources of coral

Locations where coral can be found include the Mediterranean Sea, off the coast of Australia, the South Pacific, the waters of Japan, and Africa.

Quartz crystal

Quartz crystal is a clear variety of quartz that was first found high in the frozen mountains of the Alps. Ancient people believed it was a form of ice crystals that would never melt. It is said to have cooling powers and is a romantic stone. Sources of quartz crystal include Brazil, Madagascar, Switzerland, France and parts of the Soviet Union.

Healing properties of Quartz Crystal

Crystal is a common stone, but a powerful one. It is mainly used in healing as amplification for the energies of the other working stones. In healing, the crystal point is best and the size can be important.

For meditating the crystal ball or point can be used. As it is a powerful stone the user should experiment with each to find what is best for him.

The Quartz Crystal has a similar vibration as humans. This is why using Crystal to meditate and keeping a Crystal helps one to know oneself. It will sometimes not work for a negative person.

14 Sapphire

Description: A form of corundum (as is ruby) that owes its blue colouring to traces of titanium. The colour ranges from pale to deep gentian blue as well as yellow-brown, green and violet corundums. **Enhances:** Balance of mental/spiritual/physical planes, meditation, fidelity, communication, creative expression, religious devotion, purity of mind, serenity, intellect (dark blue), selfless love (pink-violet) **Aids the maintenance or treatment of:** depression, backache, skin eruptions, tension dark blue-nerve related illnesses / bright blue heart, central nervous system, eye infections/orange- hasty reactions, irritability, spleen

Where to Wear: on finger

Chakra: brow

Zodiac: Aries / Gemini / Virgo / Capricorn / Libra

Birthstone: July

Anniversary: 23rd/65th/75th wedding anniversary

Dream: escape from danger

Care: Can be washed under luke warm water with a drop of detergent and water softener - rinse well in clear water as the soapy film can detract from the stone's lustre. Ultrasonic cleaning can lead to loss of colour.

The sky is just a gigantic blue Sapphire stone into which the earth is embedded – this belief was cherished in ancient times. And, in fact, does there exist a better image to describe the beauty of an immaculate Sapphire of purest blue? This gemstone exists in all the shades of blue skies, from the deep blue of evening skies to the bright and deep blue of a clear and beautiful summer sky which charms all people. The splendid gemstone, however, also comes in many other colours, not only in the transparent greyish misty blue of far horizons, but also displaying the bright fireworks of sunset colours – yellow, pink, orange and purple. So Sapphires are really and truly heavenly stones, although they are being found in the hard soil of our so-called "blue planet".

Blue is Sapphire's main colour. Blue is also the favourite colour of about 50 per cent of the population, men and women alike. This colour, which is strongly associated with sapphire, is also linked to emotions such as sympathy and harmony, friendship and loyalty. These emotions belong to features which are permanent and reliable – emotions where overwhelming and fiery passion is not the main element, but rather composure, mutual understanding and unshakeable trust. Sapphire blue has thus become a colour related to anything permanent and reliable, and this is one of the reasons why women in many countries settle on Sapphire for their engagement rings. Sapphire symbolises loyalty and faithfulness, while at the same time expressing love and yearning. The most famous musical example for this melancholic shade of blue can be found in George Gershwin's "Rhapsody in Blue". Sapphire's blue colour is also evoked where clear competence and controlled brainwork are the issue. After all, the first computer ever to wrangle a victory from a chess grandmaster and world champion was named "Deep Blue".

What makes Sapphire a fancy stone?

Its beauty, magnificent colours, its transparency but also its resistance and permanence are characteristics which gemstone lovers and experts assign to this gemstone – however, this does not only apply to blue Sapphire as will be pointed out later on. Sapphire belongs to the corundum group which is set apart from other gemstones by their very good hardness (Grade 9 on the Mohs' scale). They are second in hardness to diamonds only, and diamonds represent the hardest mineral on Earth! Because of their good hardness, sapphires are easy to care for as gemstones and demand from their wearers only the usual and normal care.

The corundum group consists of pure aluminium oxide, which a long time ago was caused to crystallise into beautiful and splendid gemstones by the pressure and heat in the depths of the ground. Small proportions of other elements, mainly iron and chrome, are responsible for the resulting colours and make the basically white crystals a blue, red, yellow, pink or greenish Sapphire. But this dies not necessarily imply that any corundum is a sapphire. Which stone may be termed a Sapphire – this is a question which for centuries has fuelled heated discussions among experts. Finally agreement was achieved to call ruby-red Sapphires "Rubies", and all other colours "Sapphires".

If we talk about Sapphires, most gemstone lovers will immediately think of a velvety blue. It is an adaptable colour which is attractive on many people. A blue Sapphire is optimally suited to a well-balanced style of life, where reliability is joined with spirit, and where there is an openness for new ideas and influences – just like the woman wearing it. The fact that this beautiful gemstone does also exist in many other colours was for a long time an piece of information known to insiders only. In the gemstone trade any non-blue Sapphire is termed "fancy". And to clear up matters the colour denominations are also used, so that when talking about fancy Sapphires, we talk about yellow, purple, pink, green or white Sapphire, etc. Fancy sapphires are the epitome of individualism, the perfect choice for women who love unique coloured gemstone jewellery. These Sapphires exist in a charming variety of designs - set in rings, as pendants or earrings, as solitary stones, in elegant line-ups or as sparkling pavée.

But there are even more surprises about Sapphire: for example, there is an orange colour variety with a fine pinkish undertone, which has been given the poetic name "Padparadsha", meaning "lotus flower".

Another rarity are the star Sapphires. These are stone cut in half-dome shape displaying a star-shaped light phenomenon, which seems to dance magically across the stone's surface when the Sapphire is moved. There exist rumours about gemstone lovers who have forever and truly lost their hearts to these sapphire rarities – but then, permanence and loyalty come along with these stones.

Gemological Properties

Pukhraj (Yellow Sapphire)

Chemical Composition	AL2O3 (aluminium Oxide)
Color	Any shade of yellow, from pale yellow color to dark orangish golden to greenish yellow.
Hardness	9
Refractive Index	1.762-1.770
Species	Corundum
Density	4.00
Birefringence	0.008
Occurence	Sri Lanka, Burma, Thailand, USA Cambodia, Australia, East Africa,

Astrological- Healing Properties

Pukhraj (Yellow Sapphire)

Planet	Jupiter
Cosmic Colour	Light blue
Number	3
Day	Thrusday
Time	unset

Chakra	2nd, Ajna
Red Coral Mantra	"Aum Brim brihaspataye namah" repeated 108 times at the time of wearing the yellow sapphire store.
Signs of a wellplaced Jupiter	Happiness. Good children and grand children wealth, name, fame, success and honor. Wisdom, longevity.
Signs of an afflicted Jupiter	The native will not be a moderat but an extremist. Over optimism, false hopes, careless ness, debts, disputes, failure in specu lation, gambling, pressure from credi tors, worry through children, child lessness Vanity, default, infamy, glut tony and unusual girth.
Prevention of the following diseases	Liver complaints, jaundice, dropsy flatulence, dyspepsia, abscess, dis orders of pancreas, tumors, skin troubles, cerebal congestio catarrh, circulation of blood in the arteries and fat in the body.

Gemological Properties Blue Sapphire (Neelam)

Chemical Composition	AL2O3+Fe
Color	Light blue to dark blue, violetish-blue, greenish-blue, steely-blue, color change from blue or greenish blue to violet-purple.

Hardness—9 Refractive Index—1.762-1.77	
Pleochroism	Strong dischroism
Density	Around 4
Birefringerence	0.008
Occurence	Sri Lanka, Cambodia (Pailin) Thailand, (Kanchanaburi) Burma, Kashmir, Australia (Anakie) Tanzania, Madagascar, USA (Montana, Yogo Guich)

Healing Properties Blue-Sapphire (Neelam)

Planet—Saturn Cosmic Color—Violet Number—8	
Day—Saturday Time—Sunset Chakra—4th, Arahata	
Red Coral Mantra	"Aum sham shanaiascaraya namah" repeated 23 times at the time of wearing a Saturn talisman.
Signs of a well-placed Jupiter	Wisdom, integrity, discipline, spiritual achievement through humility, patience, dedication an non-attachment. Satturn also govern leadership an perfection, highest human qualities, long life.
Signs of an afflicted Saturn	Misery, adversity, sorrows, restrictions, denials, delays, accidents, chronic diseases, theft being a thief.
Prevention of the following diseases	Paralysis, asthma, rheumatisms, teeth problems, bones problems.
Element—Air Sign—Capricorn/ Aquarius	
Sanskrit Names	Neelam, Blue sapphire, Nila-mani Blue jewel, Indra-Neelam, Royal blue gem, Sani-ratna, Saturn's gem.

15 Sapphires: Beautiful Beyond Blue

Sapphire is often considered to be synonynous with the color blue: you can easily picture sapphire seas. However, sapphire is beautiful beyond blue, in every color but red, because red is called ruby.

The other colors of sapphire can be just as beautiful and rare - or even rarer - than the blue but they are usually priced less. Yellow, orange, lavender, and other pastel shades are especially affordable.

Since our ancestors did not realize that ruby and sapphire are actually the same mineral, they left us with a dilemma: where should pink shades be classified? Long ago, people decided to call all gemstones of the mineral corundum as sapphire, except the red color, which was called ruby. But pink is really just light red. The International Colored Gemstone Association has passed a resolution that the light shades of the red hue should be included in the category ruby since it was too difficult to legislate where red ended and pink began. In practice, pink shades are now known either as pink ruby or pink sapphire. Either way, these gems are among the most beautiful of the corundum family.

Other very popular shades of fancy sapphires are yellows, bright oranges, lavender and purples, and a bluish green color.

Generally, the more clear and vivid the color, the more valuable the fancy sapphire. If the color is in the pastel range, the clarity should be good: because in lighter tones inclusions are more noticeable, the trade usually prefers the gemstones to be cleaner with fewer visible inclusions. In a lighter colored gemstone, the cut is also more important: it should reflect light back evenly across the face of the stone, making it lively and brilliant. With darker more intense colors, the cut is not as critical because the color creates its own impact.

No matter what the color, sapphires combine durability and beauty for generations of pleasure.

16 Ruby Gemstone

Description: Found in colours from pinkish to deep red, it is a Corundum (as are Sapphires) with the red colouring caused by chromium.

Enhances: amplification of energy, motivation, visualization, intuitive thinking, passion, sleep, confidence, vitality, strength, willpower.

Aids the maintenance or treatment of: heart, circulatory system, detoxification of body, blood disorders, brain, lethargy, nightmares

Special Features: Said to grow dark when danger is imminent.

Where to Wear: heart, mid chest, finger, ankle

Chakra: base / heart

Zodiac: Aries / Leo / Capricorn / Scorpio

Birthstone: July

Anniversary: 40th / 52nd wedding anniversaries **Dream:** signifies coming success in business

Care: Can be washed under luke warm water with a drop of detergent and water softener· rinse well in clear water as the soapy film can detract from the stone's lustre. Cleaning in an ultrasonic cleaner can lead to loss of colour.

Astrological- Healing

Ruby (MANAK)

Planet	Sun
Cosmic Colour	Red
Number	1

Chakra	5th, Manipura
Sun Mantra	" Aum grinih suryaya namah"
	repeated 7 times at the time of wearing a Sun talisman.
Sings of a well-placed Venus	Creative, vital, resistant, determined and decisive. Successful activity, authority. Royalty, high position in administration.
	Cheerful outlook, good fortune, ambition to achieve great height, brilliance, optimism, success in worldly affairs.
Prevention of the following diseases	Heart diseases, eye inflammation low or high blood pressure, Hem orrhage, cardiac thrombosis heated and bilious constitution Cerebral meningitis, eruption of the face, typhoid, polypus, epilepsy, bile complaints, sunstroke, scorches, diseases of the head.
Element	Fire Sign Leo
Sanskrit names	Manikya, Ruby, Padmaraga, Red lotus color gem, Shona-Ratna, Red jewel, Ravi-Ratna, Gem of the sun

Ruby-red means Passion

Red like Ruby. Ruby-red. The most important characteristic about that valuable stone is its colour. There is of course a reason for this: the name "Ruby" was derived from the Latin word "rubens" meaning "red". The red of Rubies is in a class all by otself: warm and fiery.

Precious Gemstones & Semi Precious Gemstones

Fire Agate

Fluorite

Chrysoprase

Green Topaz

Car nelian

Demantoid

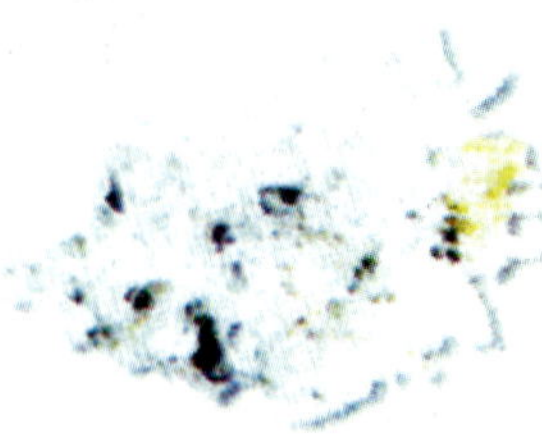

Calcite

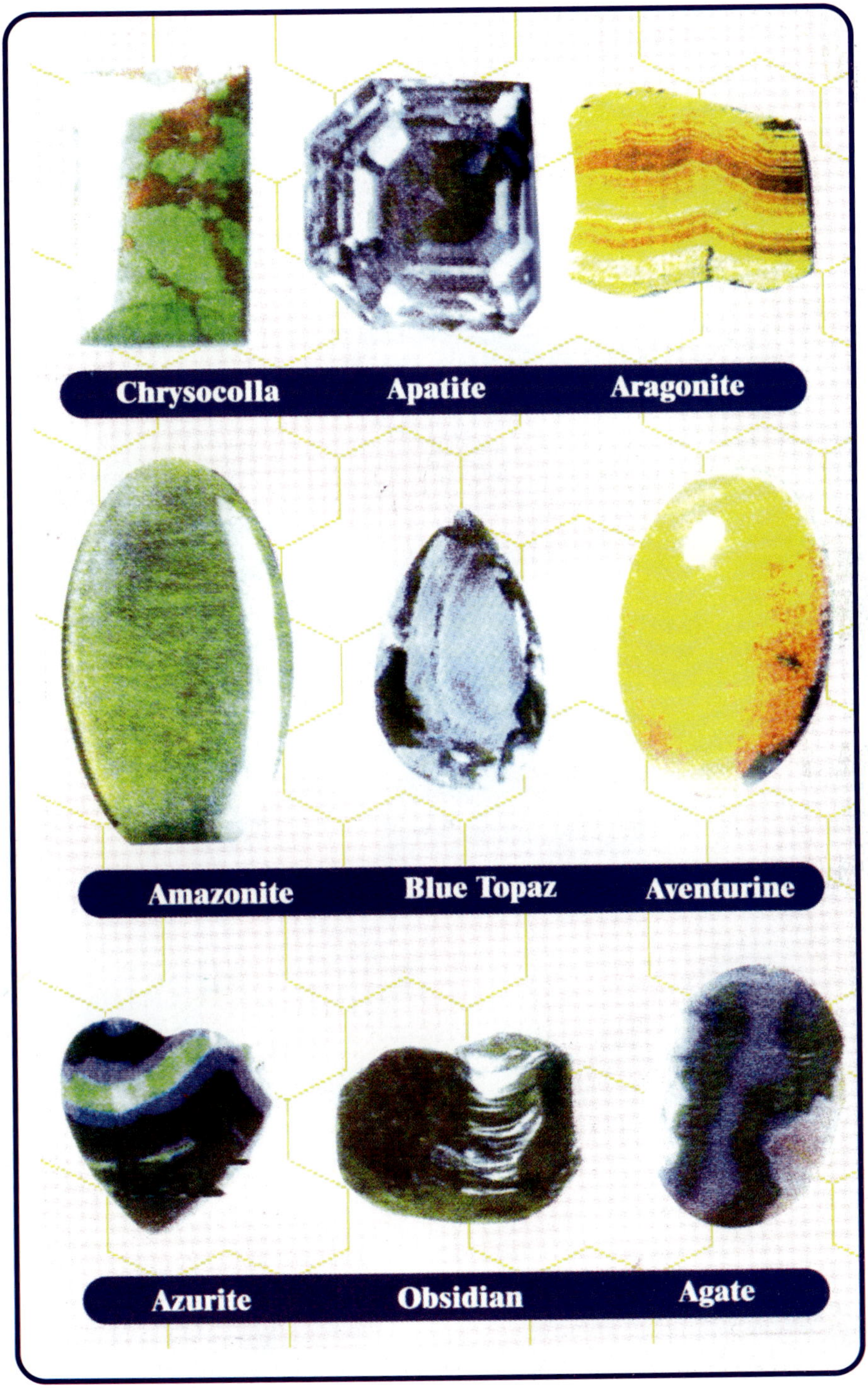
Chrysocolla
Apatite
Aragonite
Amazonite
Blue Topaz
Aventurine
Azurite
Obsidian
Agate

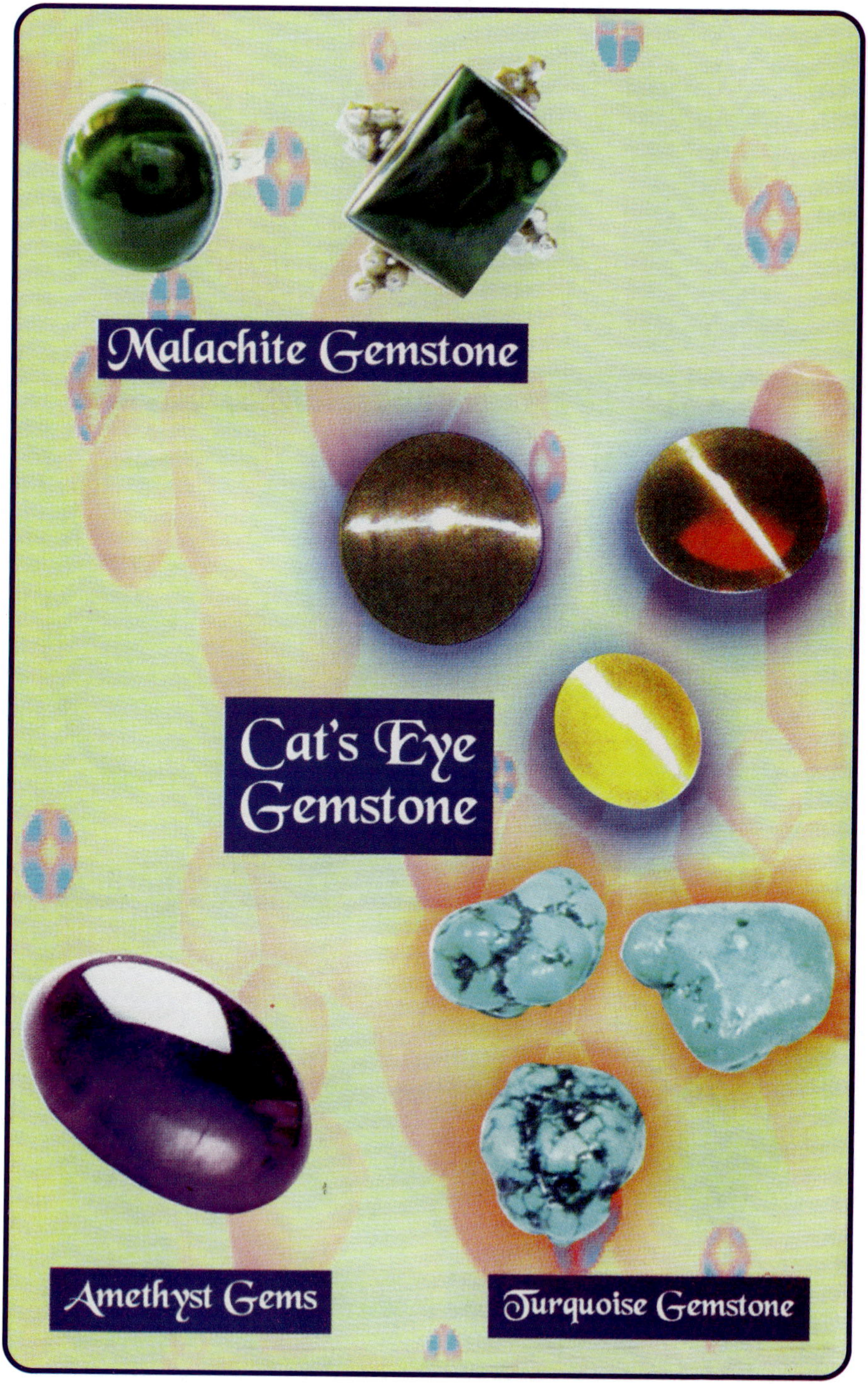
Malachite Gemstone
Cat's Eye Gemstone
Amethyst Gems
Turquoise Gemstone

Rost Quartz
Topaz
Serpentine
Sodalite
Pink Topaz
Yellow Tourmaline
Tourmaline
Zircon
Pink Sapphire

Howlite
Jasper
Green topaz
Morganite
Hematite
Rhodonite
Sapphire
Sihalite
Jet
Titanite
Jadeite
Hassonite

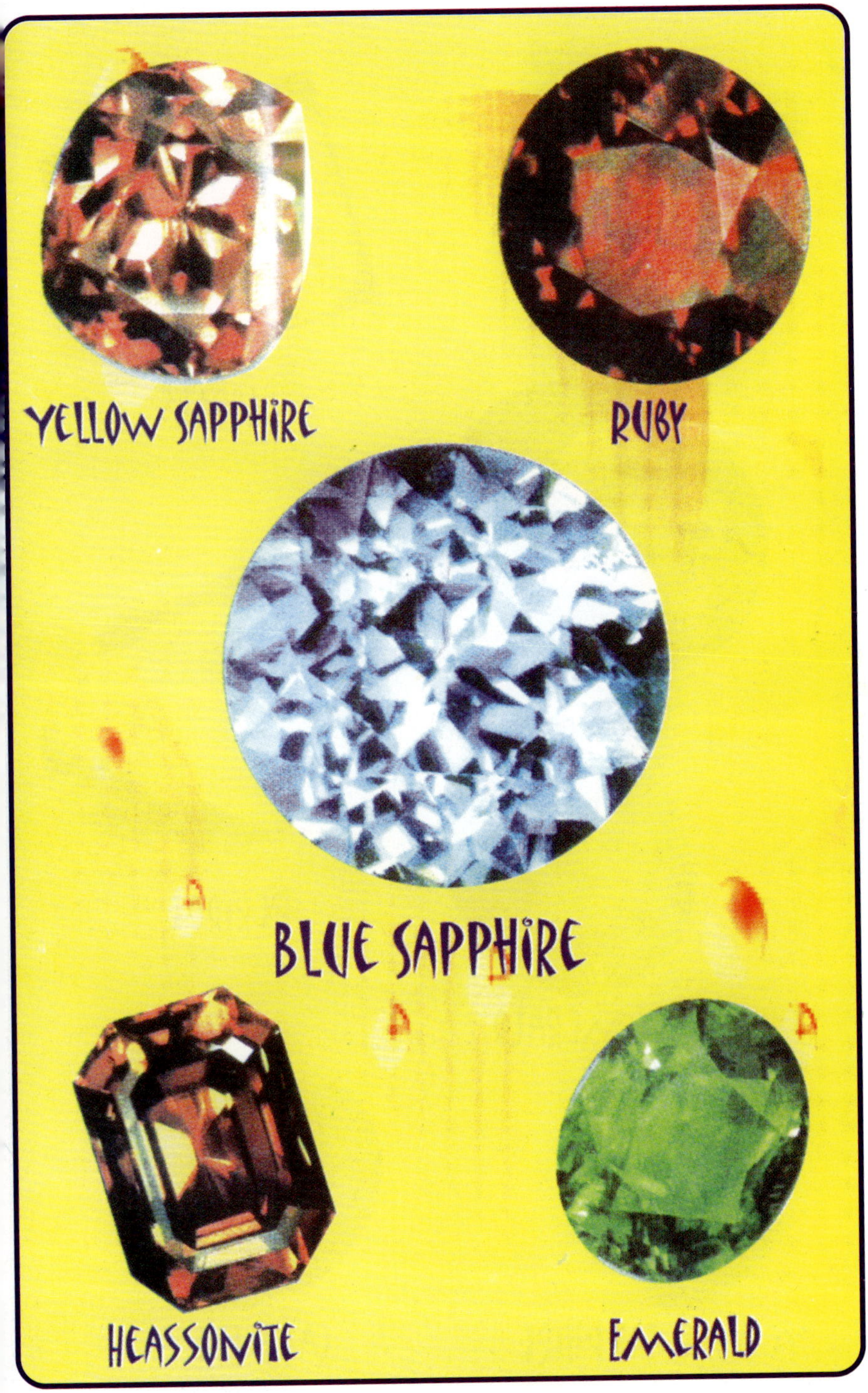
YELLOW SAPPHIRE
RUBY
BLUE SAPPHIRE
HEASSONITE
EMERALD

OPAL

CORALS

RUBY

PERIDOT

EMERALD

YELLOW SAPPHIRE

CAT'S EYE

17 Cat's Eye Gemstone

Cat's eye lets you see everything. Use the cat's eye for insight and you can be a very lucky person. When used in jewelry the cat's eye may bring good luck and protection from the evil eye to the wearer. It also known to bring clear thinking and insight.

Healing properties of Cat's Eye

Tiger's-eye or Cat's-Eye is a stone for the mind, not the body. This is a powerful stone and must be used carefully. Tiger's-eye has the power to focus the mind. It will cause the mind to have feeling of oneness and feel more direct in all thoughts. It makes one aware of one's own needs related to the needs of others. This is a very deep process and not all are capable of using the energy of the Tiger's-eye correctly.

It should be worn as a bracelet or ring set in silver and worn on the right side of the body. A personal symbol carved in Tiger's-eye is excellent for the spiritually advanced to meditate on.

Cat's eye harmonizes Ketu which is traditionally known as the " tail of the dragon". In Jyotish Ketu is the descending node of Chandra (Moon). It's influences are similar to Mangal or Mars and include liberation, abstract thinking, asceticism, non-attachment, healing, moksha- enlightenment, wisdom and that which is hidden. Ketu's influence in the Psyiology is represented by the tail of the caudate. It's influence is over learning and emotions. It's wearing removes physical weakness. Mental worries are removed. If cat's eye acts favourably, it makes one a wealthy person Gomed.

18 Topaz

Description: There are four main varieties of Topaz - yellow, pink, blue and colourless with the most common being yellow with a red tint. A classic characteristic is its perfect, lengthways cleavage.

Enhances: energy level, relaxation, creativity, individuality, confidence, sleep, balance emotions

Aids the maintenance or treatment of: nervous system, tension, blood, negativity, high blood pressure, insomnia, throat disorders, depression, anger, disturbed emotions, digestive system, cleansing organs, thyroid, metabolism, arthritis pain

Special Features: This stone makes an excellent pocket companion.

Where to Wear: best as a ring Chakra: heart / throat, brow

Zodiac: Aries / Leo / Sagittarius / Gemini

Birthstone: November

Dream: signifies safety from harm

Care: Can be washed under luke warm water with a drop of detergent and water softener - rinse well in clear water as the soapy film can detract from the stone's lustre. Ultrasonic cleaning can lead to a loss of colour.

Topaz has low dispersio n and a cleavage perfect in one direction. Topaz is recommended for those whose solar sign is Gemini? It can also be worn by those under the signs of Libra and Scorpio.

Topazes can be orange- yellow, amber- gold, blue, purple, the colour of sherry, brown, or pink. The most· valuable topaz is known as Imperial topaz, and it is reddish gold. The pink and pea c h (brownish yellow) topazes are more costly than other colors. Blue topaz is the most common and the least expensive. Blue topaz comes mainly from China. It is colourless or white when it is mined, but irradiation changes the stone to an electric blue. If this is done improperly, the gem can become radioactive, and it is not recommended for astrological use when irradiated. Other topazes are found in Brazil, Russia, Ukraine and Pakistan.

Topaz is a hard gem, but it cleaves easily, so a hard blow can crack it. A sudden change in temperature can also cause topaz to crack.

Topaz can have a good influence over the mind and soul. It helps one become more aware, happier, creative, improve one's concentration, increases one's intelligence, and helps one have better clarity of mind. It helps improve wealth, relieves depression, and helps one avoid misfortune. Topaz can help those with dangerous jobs, and can help make life more pleasant. It also helps a couple remain loyal to one another.

Topaz works with the nervous system, relieves exhaustion, mental problems, and diseases of the solar plexus. It can help cure heart complications, migraines, liver problems, diarrhoea, rheumatism, ulcers, insomnia, arthritis, jaundice, impotency, and gout.

Appearance: Often found in short to long prismatic crystals, sometimes with characteristic terminal faces. It is often white, semi opaque, milky, or tinged a dirty yellow, but may be transparent, colourless, honey coloured, golden brown, brown or blue; much more rarely pink or reddish. The transparent, coloured crystals, which also have good luster, are widely used as gems.

Physical Properties: It has a hardness of 8 and a density of 3.52-3.56 g/cm3. The density and refractive indices are interrelated and depend on the composition of the specimen: topazes richest in hydroxyl (OR) have a low density and high refractive indices, whereas those richest in fluorine have a higher density and low refractive indices. The stone has easy perfect basal cleavage.

Genesis: Topaz is characteristic of pegmatitic and pneumatolytic deposits and is therefore found in dykes and contact aureoles around grantic intrusiolli. It is also found in alluvial deposits, but is, perhaps. the most vulnerable of the harder gemstones to anac.k by the elements, at least in tropical or equatorial regions.

Occurrence: The mineral first classified scientifically' as topaz came from Saxony. The topazes of Brazil are famous, some being of gigantic proportions. Topazes are also found in Mexico, the United States, Sri Lanka. Japan, the Soviet Union (both in Silberia and in the Urals), Nigeria, and Zaire, to mention just the main sources.

Topaz Gemstone

Topaz is one of the twelve breastplate stones of the High Priest referred to in the Book of Exodus. The breastplate stones are considered sacred to twelve mighty angels who guard the gates to Paradise.

Topaz occurs in several colors. This is a lovely white or clear topaz from the Geraes mine in Brazil.

White Topaz:

- Increases your awareness of thoughts and deeds and the karmic effects of these
- Purifies emotions as well as actions
- Activates cosmic awareness
- Removes stagnant energy

Topaz Meaning

Topaz is a soothing, empathetic stone that will direct energy to the place it is most needed. It heals and energizes. Topaz is a promoter of truth and forgiveness. Use it to find your own path.

Sources Topaz

Topaz occurs in a range of different colors: deep golden yellow (Imperial Topaz), blue, light to medium brown (Champagne Topaz), pink, and white, or clear topaz.

Topaz can be found in Brazil, USA, Sri Lankooa, Myanmar, former USSR, Australia, Tasmania, Pakistan, Mexico, Japan and Africa.

19 Yellow Topaz

True topaz or yellow topaz is the most typical variety, and no adjectives are needed to describe its colour, although different shades are sometimes referred to as "golden topaz" or "sherry topaz".

Appearance: The colour can range from golden to honey yellow or can be golden brown or honey with a pink or reddish tinge. The crystals are usually cut into oval gems but pear and other mainly elongated shapes are also produced, usually with a crown and pavilion consisting of very many small lozenge-shaped facts, which bring out the luster of the stone. The longer stones often look darker at the ends. Easy basal cleavage makes these gems rather brittle so they should be treated with care and protected from the type of sharp blows to which ring stones are susceptible. Medium-large stones are relatively common, and even very large ones are not rare.

Distinctive features : A great deal of citrine quartz, which looks fairly similar, is sold under the name of topaz or topaz citrine, creating some confusion on the market. The color of topaz is however, generally much warmer and more likely to have an orange or pinkish tone. The stone will also have a much greater luster. In any event, a quick check of the density, perhaps using one of the heavy liquids, would immediately distinguish between the two, and measurement of the refractive indices would remove all trace of doubt.

Occurrence: Topaz comes mainly from Brazil, and in smaller quantities, from the Soviet Union, Japan, Sri Lanka, Burma, and the United States. It is occasionally found in Germany.

Value: Well coloured, medium-large specimens of true topaz are quite valuable, but perhaps less so today than in the past. Roughly on a par with secondary gemstones, such as the better tourmalines, it has probably suffered from the ready availability of citrine quartz, an inferior stone, which, by usurping the name, has made topaz seem more abundant than it really is.

Simultants and synthetics: The main problem is the practice of passing citrine quartz off as topaz. Synthetic corundum of a colour similar to topaz has also been produced by way of imitation, whereas topaz itself has only been synthesized on a limited scale for scientific purposes and is not found on the market.

Yellow Topaz is inexpensive but can work wonders. Yellow Topaz is highly recommended for those belonging to solar sign Gemini. Yellow Topaz can also be used with profit by Librans and Scorpios. According to ancient Hindu mythology use of this gem, ward off the risk to injury or attack. Yellow Topaz should be used by those duties involve handling of dangerous machines. Yellow Topaz works as a talisman to cure certain diseases including mental deerangemtn, hysterai madness, suicidal tendency.

Yellow Topaz symbolizes sobriety, clemency, faithfullness, and gentleness. One gets kindhearted, generosu and wealthy by wearing Yellow Topaz. One also get more brilliancy and intellignece leading a peaceful, pleasant and contended life. The spouse of the wearer will be faithfull and loyal forever. Yellow Topaz is also recommended gem for persons of birth number 1. The use of Yellow Topaz gem also appeases anger, turns sadness into happiness, brings wealth and enhances positions and prestige. Yellow Topaz should be used in combination with pearl of good quality. (In addition Sri yantra carved or silver or cooer or gold ring should be used which will enhance the efficacy of the use of the precious gem) Use of this gem facilitates recovery of lost possessions and improvement in financial status and position. It also confers dignity, poise, intelligence, wisdom and nobility of character. Its use is recommended for those suffering from cough and cold, liver ailments, jaundice, nervious disorders, loss of appetite, indisgestion, burning sensation in limbs leprosy.

20 Pink Topaz

As already mentioned, true or yellow topaz may be pinkish orange or yellow with a pink tinge. There is in fact a whole range of color gradations from yellow to pink, and it is hard to establish a dividing line between the two varieties.

Appearance: In some cases the colour is pink with a distinctive yellowish or orange shade, but it is more often a definite light to medium pink, tending to red or violet in deeper coloured stones. The colour is not always evenly distributed and can show slight crystallographic zoning. The stones usually have few inclusions and are strongly transparent and lustrous.

The most common cut is the oval or pear shape, but many other old or antique faceted cuts are seen, as is the step cut. While it has always been comparatively rare, pink topaz was much appreciated in antique jewelry and stones weighing up to 10 carats are often found.

Distinctive features: At first sight, there is not much difference between pink topaz, kunzite, morganite, and some pink tourmalines. But a density test with a heavy liquid such as methylene iodide, in which topaz sink but the others float, will distinguish topaz from the others. It is corundum, the former having about the same density as topaz, and the latter having a highly density. In case of confusion with these stones, other properties, such as the refractive indices, need to 1 examined.

Occurrence: Pink topaz comes mainly from Brazil, but has also been mined recently in the Ural mountains of the Soviet Union. In both places, intensely coloured reddish or purplish specimens have very occasionally been found.

Value: When the colour is fairly intense, it is one of the IT valuable of the second level gemstones (e.g. aquamarine Specimens that are too pale have a low value. Like yellow topaz, it perhaps more highly prized in past than today.

21 Blue Topaz

This is the variety of topaz most readily available in the market today.

Appearance: It has a definite, uniform sky-blue colour usually without any overtones. Often pale, it can be bright or very rarely an intense blue. It sometimes has a slight gray or even greenish tinge, giving it a lifeless appearance. Gemstones of several carats or even several tens of carats in weight are relatively common Furthermore, they are usually wholly or almost free of inclusions. This is often the case where large amounts of material of no great value are available; the less clear pieces are discarded. The most common cut is the oval, with the crown and pavilion consisting of very many lozenge-shaped facets, but all the mixed cuts, plus the step cut, are used. As with all light-colored gemstones, the value of blue topaz increases with intensity of color, provided this is attractive and not somber. Like other types of topaz, it cleaves readily and this can affect its durability.

Distinctive features: There is, at first sight, some resemblance to aquamarine; but close observation will distinguish the two, as aquamarine always displays a very attractive pleochrosm from blue to greenish blue of even bluish green. Topaz is usually a more definite blue, if anything with a grayish tone, which certainly distinguishes it from aquamarine. Measurement of the density alone is not enough to distinguish topaz from synthetic blue spinel, which can be very similar in colour. Before measuring other physical properties, such as the refractive indices, the stone can be examined under a lens for signs of birefringence. Although faint, a doubling of the facet edges will be visible in topaz. If this is present, one can immediately rule out the possibility of its being synthetic spinel or glass, both of which are singly refractive.

Occurrence: Blue topaz is found in various parts of Brazil, Mexico, and the United States. It is mined in Burma (in the Mogok region, famous for rubies) and the Soviet Union (chiefly in the Urals and the Kamchatka peninsula). It is also found in Namibia and Nigeria.

22 Colourless Topaz

As a mineral, this is far and away the most common variety of transparent topaz, although it is of limited importance as a gemstone. All colourless gemstones compare most unfavourably with diamond, their lower refractive indices and lesser dispersion making them far less attractive. Topaz has the advantage over the others of being found in large stones and great quantities, and of having good hardness and luster. Therefore it is of some interest to hobbyists.

Appearance: Gemstones are generally free, or almost so, quantities available; but they may show signs of extensive internal cleavage. In large stones (of a few centimeters) the of a lens, the facet edges appearing double when seen good luster and are only disappointing on the rare occasions when they are given the brilliant cut, prompting comparison with diamonds. which have a very different luster and "fire."

Distinctive features: topaz differs little from the colourless varieties of other minor gems, which, with the exception of quartz, are all much rarer; incipient cleavage, where present, may be a distinguishing feature. If the edges appear double, denoting birefringence, this can distinguish it from synthetic colorless spinel, which has a similar density, but it cannot differentiate it from other minor gemstones such as colorless beryl, tourmaline, and corundum. To distinguish it with any certainly from these. the refractive indices must be determined.

Occurrence: It is found in various parts of Brazil. the Soviet Union, the United States, Germany (Saxony) and Japan. Mrica too has a plentiful supply of colorless topaz in the tin-mining areas of both Nigeria and Zaire It is also found in Namibia.

Simulants and synthetics: It is neither imitated nor produced synthetically.

23 Imperial Topaz Gemstone

Topaz is one of the twelve breastplate stones of the High Priest referred to in the Book of Exodus. The breastplate stones are considered sacred to twelve mighty angels who guard the gates to Paradise.

Today, imperial topaz is used to:

- Encourage self realization and confidence
- Impart strength to quiet wild emotions
- Banish bad dreams
- Bestow charisma on its user
- Topaz draws love to its wearer
- Protection against envy, disease, negative magic and sudden or untimely death
- Combined with an equal amount of tiger eye, topaz will bring wealth and money

Healing properties of Imperial Topaz

- Stimulate the appetite
- Aid in nervous exhaustion
- Activate life force and metabolism

Sources of Imperial Topaz

Topaz occurs in a range of different colors: deep golden yellow (Imperial Topaz), blue, light to medium brown (Champagne Topaz), pink, and white topaz.

Topaz can be found in Brazil, USA, Sri Lanka, Myanmar, former USSR, Australia, Tasmania, Pakistan, Mexico, Japan and Africa.

24 Astrological Gems

The use of gemstones and crystals for psychic as well as decorative purposes is now widespread. Do these gemstones have any astrological significance, and if so, how does one work out which stones to use for best effect?

As a general rule, the best benefits can be obtained by wearing or using the stones represented by the strongest or most favourably aspected planets in your natal chart. It is, after all, those planets which tend to indicate the characteristics that we are most 'at home with' within ourselves. A common mistake is for someone to wear or to use a stone associated with a quality they wish to possess or enhance, but which is not naturally assimilated by them. Rather than the gemstone being able to endow us with some mystical quality which we lack, it is far better to view them as tools to enhance the abilities we already possess - and thereby making us in a stronger position to seek within ourselves for the qualities we wish to develop.

The following list will be of use in selecting which stones may work well for you as an individual. When the term well-aspected is used, I mean a planet which is strong by exaltation, rulership, house position and/or in favourable aspect to the 'benefics' i.e. Venus or Jupiter. If you do not know which are the strongest planets in your chart, any astrologer should be able to tell you quickly and simply.

When the SUN is well aspected:

Amber, fluorite and chrysolite are recommended. Amber (actually a fossilised resin, rather than a 'gem') certainly conveys a sunny colour, but is also helpful in creating balance in life and in making space for spiritual aims as well as materialistic ones. It absorbs negativity, and has a general harmonising influence. Physically, it is said to benefit the conditions of stress, asthma and urinary problems.

Fluorite is another powerful healer, which has specific applications in the well-being of teeth, gums and bones. Chrysolite is reputed to be powerful in healing viral illness, toxaemia and appendix problems.

When the MOON is well aspected:

Moonstone, quartz (especially milky quartz), emerald and carnelian are recommended. The Moonstone is well known as a soothing influence on troubled emotions, as well as an aid to intuition and the understanding of dreams. Milky quartz absorbs excess mental and emotional energy and has a general calming influence.

Emerald was used in ancient times to cure eye disorders, but is also said to enhance one's courage and self-esteem. Carnelian is perhaps best known for increasing fluency both of speech and of ideas - this stone is of especial benefit to anyone in the public eye.

When MERCURY is well aspected:

Moss agate and banded agate are recommended. Both of these stones are said to attract loyalty and to cushion the user from harmful vibrations. The agate stones have a very earthy, grounding influence, which can be invaluable to the Mercurial personality. They also promote both truth and strength.

When VENUS is well aspected:

Opal, Lapis Lazuli, Coral and Green Jasper are recommended. Physically, the Opal is said to increase the assimilation of protein into the body and to be helpful to the lungs. The Opal is an important stone and also represents unconditional love such as that of a parent to a child. It is important that this stone is not worn by anyone with an afflicted (difficultly aspected) Venus.

Lapis Lazuli is often known as the third eye stone, reputed to help inner vision and enhance psychic abilities. This stone is also found to be helpful in decision making. Coral (not technically a gemstone) is primarily known for strengthening the spleen, whilst it's other main physical attribute is to aid the treatment of the voice and throat. Green Jasper is a stabilising stone which calms ad steadies the emotions. It is also said to be a remedy for ulcers.

When MARS is well aspected:

Bloodstone, Smoky Quartz and Diamond are recommended. The diamond is a stone of Mars-like strength and courage, said to give clarity of ambition and the determination to resist setbacks. Diamond also, however, has the capacity to magnify negative thoughts and vibrations, and should be used with care. The Bloodstone is said to purify the blood, and is a useful stone to wear next to the body if the wearer is suffering physical trauma.

Smoky Quartz is a powerful healing crystal and a grounder of excess energy. It is also traditionally said to increase fertility in both sexes. In days gone by it was given to soldiers as a good luck token, as it is also believed to protect the wearer or carrier from danger.

When JUPITER is well aspected:

Topaz is recommended. This stone is said to calm the mind and to bring refreshing sleep. Kidney and bladder complaints and the treatment of varicose veins are also associated with this stone.

When SATURN is well aspected:

Onyx and Malachite are recommended. Onyx, especially black onyx is said to help overcome hearing problems and to promote concentration and self-control. Malachite, with its high copper content, is said to be beneficial against menstrual cramps and rheumatism.

When URANUS is well aspected:

Zircon and Garnet are recommended. Tourmaline is also sometimes associated with Uranus due to its highly electrical properties.

Zircon has physical applications in the aiding of childbirth and the treatment of insomnia. It is also said to aid spiritual insight. The Garnet's main uses are in the treatment of blood disorders, however this popular stone is also said to forewarn it's wearer of impending danger by losing some of its colour. Energy, beauty and new opportunities are also said to await its wearer.

When NEPTUNE is well aspected:

Amethyst and Aquamarine are recommended. The Amethyst is a marvellous and beautiful stone, widely used for meditation and healing applications. It is said to increase intuition and to promote psychic development. It is also very helpful in relieving sleeplessness and headaches. Aquamarine prevents water-retention and is said to be a good aid to the eyesight.

When PLUTO is well aspected:

Magnetite (lodestone) and Beryl are recommended. Magnetite is an energy restorer and has applications in the treatment of liver problems. It is also said to stimulate the whole endocrine system, and is a useful stone for meditation.

Beryl is the 'original' crystal in as much as it is probably this stone that was used by the ancients for srcying. It stimulates deep seated psychic abilities and clairvoyance, and is also said to increase the will power. The elimination of things that have served their purpose is said to be encouraged by this stone.

Many of the stones mentioned in this piece are not widely known to the lay-person, and you may not be aware of what they look like. Surprisingly enough, the best advice of all, if you want to try some crystal therapy, is to find a good crystal shop and to spend some time looking at and handling the various stones (a good, professional store owner won't mind this at all, in fact they will probably encourage it). Make your final choice based on which stone you feel most drawn to - when you have made your choice, that stone strikingly often turns out to be one of those most associated with your strongest planet.

25 Gemstone And Disease

Ayurveda mentions Mani (Gemstones), Mantra and Medicine are all useful to cure disease and to maintain sound health. As per Ayurveda there are seven elements in body that maintain good health and are cause of growth of body and different disease. The seven planets Sun, Moon, Mercury, Jupiter, Venus, Saturn control these seven element. Almost all the gems have some kind of medicinal properties. But the jewels that belong to **Navratna category** are famous for their medicinal properties as well besides their divine virtues. Treatment of a particular disease with the help of a gemstone is known as **Gemopathy.**

Ruby Gemstone increases vitality of the body and built immune power of the body system. It has positive effect on heart and it reduces the chances of back pain, eye trouble, and fire accident, gastric and peptic ulcer. It is said that the ladies should avoid it as it destroy the luster of the body.

Pearl has effect on mind and it controls the mental disease such as insomnia, poor memory. It gives peace of mind. It controls the disease of lungs, breast, heart, diabetes, piles, diarrhea, deficiency of calcium. Pearl is useful for ladies as it increase the luster of face and increase the strength of sex. It makes their conjugal life happy.

Red Coral gemstone controls the aggressive behavior of individual. It may protect from accidents, injuries, and wounds. It has good effects on control of menstrual disorders, reduce the chance of miscarriage and make safe delivery. **Emerald** gemstone increases brainpower, intelligence, reasoning ability, communication skill, and speech power. It reduces passion and sexual desire. It can be used to control trouble related to asthma, skin, and bronchitis.

Yellow Sapphire gemstone controls the functioning of liver, jaundice, anemia, blood pressure, and gastric trouble, fever.

Diamond has good effects on the private parts and sex organs. It cure sexual weakness, kidney trouble, diabetes.

Blue Sapphire is positive effects on nervous and joint disorder and control gastric trouble, gout, arthritis, heart trouble, asthma, and legs pain. It increases stamina. It improves the fertility of barren women.

Hessonite (Gomed) gemstone controls indigestion, skin disease, insomnia, hysteria, snakeobite, dog-bite, blood poisoning. It also control undiagnosed disease.

Cats Eye gemstone is very hot in nature and cure paralysis, mania, blood poisoning, malignant disease, undiagnosed disease.

GEM	**DISEASE**
Ruby	Heart disorders, hallucination, fear, confusion, eye disorders etc.
Pearl:	Blood disorders, semetic disorders, mental instability, abdominal diseases.
Coral:	Insanity, epilepsy, coma, hallucinations and disorders of the brain.
Emerald:	Loss of voice, insomnia, effects of poison, skin diseases and insomnia.
Yellow Sapphire	Lethargy, heaviness, liver disorders, breast-related diseases.
Diamond:	Mouth diseases, impotency, loss of voice, semetic disorders etc.
Blue Sapphire	Insanity, wind diseases, abdominal disorders, infertility.

HOW TO WEAR THE STONE - To obtain the full benefic effects of stone, wear it while Moon is waxing on the specified day & time. Wearing it in the specified Nakshatra enhances the benefic effects of the stone. Take the stone of a size specified or greater in fractions of 1/4 Ratti rejecting fractions of 3/4 Ratti like 4-1/4 Ratti. Get it studded in the specified metal such that it touches the finger from bottom. The Gem before weraring to be energiged with rituals and must be worn on auspicious Muhurta.

Stone	Planet	Weight	Metal	Finger	Day	Time	Nakshatra
RUBY	SUN	3 RATTI	GOLD	RING	SUN	MORNING	KRITTIKA, U PHAL, U SHAD
PEARL	MON	3 RATTI	SILVER	LITTLE	MON	MORNING	ROHINI, HASTA, SRAVANA
CORAL	MAR	6 RATTI	SILVER	RING	MAR	MORNING	MRGSHRA, CHITRA, DHANISHTA
EMERALD	MER	4 RATTI	GOLD	LITTLE	MER	MORNING	ASHLESHA, JYESHTHA, REVATI
YELLOW SAPH	JUP	4 RATTI	GOLD	FIRST	JUP	MORNING	PUNRAVASU, VISHAKHA, P BHA
DIAMOND	VEN	1/4 RATTI	PLATINUM	LITTLE	VEN	MORNING	BHARANI, P PHAL, P SHADA
BLUE SAPH	SAT	4 RATTI	5-METAL	MIDDLE	SAT	EVENING	PUSHYA, ANURADHA, U BHAD
GOMED	RAH	5 RATTI	8-METAL	MIDDLE	SAT	NIGHT	ARDRA, SWATI, SHATBHISHA
CAT'S EYE	KET	6 RATTI	SILVER	RING	JUP	NIGHT	ASHWANI, MAGHA, MOOLA

Stone	Mantra	Contradictory Stone	Items
RUBY	ॐ घृणिः सूर्याय नमः।	DIAMOND, B SAPH, GOMED	WHEAT,SANDAL,GHEE,RED CLOTH
PEARL	ॐ सों सोमाय नमः।	GOMED	RICE,SUGAR,CURD,WHITE CLOTH
CORAL	ॐ अं अंगारकाय नमः।	DIAMOND, GOMED, B SAPH	WHEAT,COPPER,GUR, RED CLOTH
EMERALD	ॐ बुं बुधाय नमः।	--------	MOONG, BRONZE, GREEN CLOTH
Y SAPH	ॐ वृं वृहस्पतये नमः।	DIAMOND, B SAPH	GRAM PULSE,GUR,YELLOW CLOTH
DIAMOND	ॐ शुं शुक्राय नमः।	RUBY, CORAL, Y SAPH	RICE, SILVER, WHITE CLOTH
B SAPH	ॐ शं शनैश्चराय नमः।	RUBY, CORAL, Y SAPH	HORSE BEAN,OIL, BLACK CLOTH
GOMED	ॐ रां राहवे नमः।	RUBY, PEARL, CORAL	MOLE, OIL, LEAD, BLUE CLOTH
CAT EYE	ॐ कें केतवे नमः।	--------	7 CORNS,COCONUT,BROWN CLOTH

Planet	Main Gems	Direction	Alternative Gems	Colour	Metal
Budh	EMERALD	North East	Peridot, green tourmaline, chrysoprase	Green	Gold
Sukra	DIAMOND	East	White sapphire, white zircon	White	Sil., G, Plat.
Chandra	PEARL	South East	Moonstone	White	Sil., Plat.
Guru	YELLOW SAPPHIRE	North	Yellow topaz, scapolite, heliodor	Yellow	Gold
Surya	RUBY	Centre (House)	Red garnet (umbalite, rhodolite), red tourmaline, red spinel	Dark Pink	Gold
Mangal	RED CORAL	South	Carnelian	Red	Gold + Copper 18 Ct.
Ketu	CAT'S EYE chrysoberyl	North West	cat's eye quartz, cat's eye tourmaline	Gray Brown	5 Metals
Shani	BLUE SAPPHIRE	West	Amethyst, blue spinel, lapis lazuli	Dark Blue	5 Metals
Rahu	HESSONITE	South West	Orange zircon	Brown	5 or 7 Metals

<u>Gems Prescription on the basis of 'Janma Nakshatra'-the 'Birth Constellation'</u> - In this system the Gemstones prescription is based on the constellation (Nakshatra) rising at the time of birth.

NAKSHATRA	RULING PLANET	GEMSTONE
ASWINI	KETU	CAT'S EYE
BHARANI	VENUS	DIAMOND
KRITTIKA	SUN	RUBY
ROHINI	MOON	PEARL
MRIGSHIRA	MARS	RED CORAL
ADRA	RAHU	HESSONITE
PUNARVASU	JUPITER	YELLOW SAPPHIRE
PUSHYAMI	SATURN	BLUE SAPPHIRE
ASHLESHA	MERCURY	EMERALD
MAGHA	KETU	CAT'S EYE
POORVA PHALGUNI	VENUS	DIAMOND
UTTRA PHALGUNI	SUN	RUBY
HASTA	MOON	PEARL
CHITRA	MARS	RED CORAL
SWATI	RAHU	HESSONITE
VISHAKA	JUPITER	YELLOW SAPPHIRE
ANURADHA	SATURN	BLUE SAPPHIRE
JYESHTA	MERCURY	EMERALD

NAKSHATRA	RULING PLANET	GEMSTONE
MOOLA	KETU	CAT'S EYE
POORVASHADA	VENUS	DIAMOND
UTTARASHADA	SUN	RUBY
SRAVANA	MOON	PEARL
DHANISHTA	MARS	RED CORAL
POORV BHADRAPAD	JUPITER	YELLOW SAPPHIRE
UTTRA BHADRAPAD	SATURN	BLUE SAPPHIRE
REVATHI	MERCURY	EMERALD

Gems Prescription on the basis of First alphabet of the Name :

In this system the gemstones are prescribed on the basis of the first alphabet of the name of the person as per Indian sound of pronunciation of that letter. The table below gives the bird's eye view of details of the system.

FIRST LETTER OF NAME	LORD OF THE	RECOM
Choo,chey,cho,laa,lee,loo,leylow,aa	Mars Aries	Red Coral
Ee,oo,ey,o,vaa,vee,voo,vey,vo	Venus Taurus	Diamond
Kaa,kee,koo,ghau,ddau,chhau,ke,ko,haa	Mercury Gemini	Emerald
Hee,hoo,hey,ho,ddaa,ddee,ddoo,ddey,ddo,aa	Moon Cancer	Pearl
Maa,mee,moo,mey,mo,ttaa,ttee,ttoo,ttey	Sun Leo	Ruby
Tto,paa,pee,po,poo,pey,shshau,nnhau,tthau	Mercury Virgo	Emerald
Raa,ree,roo,rey,ro,thaa,thee,thoo,tey	Venus Libra	Diamond
Tho,naa,nee,noo,ney,no,yaa,yee	Mars Scorpio	Red Coral
Yey,yo,bhaa,bhee,bhoo,dhau,phaa,ddaa,bhey	Jupiter Sagittarius	Yellow Sapphire
Bho,jaa,jee,khee,khoo,khey,kho,gaa,gee	Saturn Capricorn	Blue Sapphire
Goo,gey,go,saa,see,loo,ley,low,aa	Saturn Aquarius	Blue Sapphire
Dhee,dhoo,thaw,jhaw,bhaw,dhey.chaa,chee	Jupiter Pisces	Yellow Sapphire

26 Precious Gems Their Mystical And Divine Powers

The nine precious stones are Ruby, Pearl, Yellow, Sapphire, Diamond, Emerald, Blue Sapphire, Red Coral, Gomeda and Cat's Eye.

1. Ruby:

is the stone of the sun, and wearing of Ruby will protect the native from the harmful effects of sun's afflictions. Ruby is in red colour, yellow colour, violet mixed red colour, and in rose colour. Wearing of a Ruby will give intelligence and knowledge. The subject would be blessed with children, honoured by others, and receive government favour. Ruby wil bestow mental peace, success in politics, educational fields gains of land and property, comfort of conveyances. Ruby will protect one from ill-health, enemies success in administrative fields, freedom from troubles, debts and diseases. It ensures long life, and cures heart diseases.

Note: Persons born on 8, 17, 26, 6, 15 & 24 should not wear Ruby.

2. Pearl:

Pearls are available in many colours, but of all the colours, white and red coloured pearls are the best pearls. Round pearls are superior. Flat typed pearls should not be worn. Wearing of Pearl helps the native get freedom from mental disturbances, happiness from mother, success in educational fields, gain of landed and house property and conveyances., Pearl ensures good health and long life. It improves finance. With its help one can achieve name, fame and is blessed with male children. It brings success in career, and removes evil effects of bad spirits. Pearl will even bring together a separated couple. It drives away bad luck and ensures good luck. Cures mental disorder,· gastric disorder, asthma, cough, eye trouble, and breathing troubles and lung disorder.

Note: Pearl should not be worn by persons born on 3, 12, 21, 30, 8, 17, 26 dates.

3. Yellow Sapphire:

It is available in light yellow or golden colour. It should be heavy, transparent and glittering. Yellow sapphire will make one intellectual, charitable, religiously inclined and respectable towards elders. It ensures wealth, honours, name and fame. It will bless the native with good children. It also acts as A protective charm. It ensures comforts in life. One can fulfil all the desires by wearing yellow sapphire. Those who find obstruction in the progress of their educational field, or those who suffer from property matters should wear yellow sapphire for removal for their difficulties.

Note: Yellow Sapphire should not be worn by persons born on dates 2, 11, 20, 29, 5, 14, 23,6, 15, 24, 7, 16, 25, 8, 17, 26

4. Emerald:

This is a beautiful velvety green colour stone. The Emerald with a deep velvet green to grass green colour, radiant, smooth, transparent and with bright rays, with water mark, and without any dots or spots, is the best and most auspicious gem.

Emerald helps in acquiring wealth and the native would be blessed with children, intelligence and good fortune. It also bestows good health, wealth, 'longevity, lands and property, domestic happiness, a smooth and obstruction-free life. It brings advancement in profession, name, fame and honour.

drives away evil spirits.

cures eye diseases.

controls B.P. and nervous problems.

turns enemies into friends.

Note: Emerald should not be worn by persons born on dates 3, 12, 1, 30, 9, 18, 27.

. Diamond:

Diamonds are white, blue, red and black colour stones. It. ensures ongevity, and advancement in life. It can bless the native with children, appiness, inteligence, name, fame arid good fortune. It ensures bundant wealth, and success in all ventures.

It cures the diseases of kidney and reproductive organs. It drives away evil spirits, lilt! bad effects of evil eyes. It ensures happy married life, possession of jewellery and and ornaments, rich dresses, onveyance, comfortable house, birrh of good children etc.

Note: Diamond should not be worn by persons born on dates 1, 10, 9, 28, 3, 12, 21, 30, 9, 18, 27.

. Red Coral:

Red Coral as its name suggests is generally of red colour. It may even be of orange red colour.

Red Coral will bestow good health, longevity, courage, name, fame and happiness. The native would be blessed with children, intelligence, good fortune and success in professional life. It would also grant land and property, domestic harmony, gains of wealth. It cures all kinds of mental diseases, physical diseases, and difficulties. It saves one from natural calamities like thunder, floods and fires. Its use also helps in removing impediments that could be delaying one's marriage.

Women who go in for abortions should wear this for successful delivery.

Note: Red coral should not be worn by persons born on dates 2, 11, 20,29,5, 14,23,7,15,25,8, 17,26.

7. Blue Sapphire:

This is available in dark, ordinary, or light blue colours. Blue sapphire is ruled by Saturn. It is believed that it gives very beneficial results. But in case it proves unsuitable, it could destroy the life of the native. It has been experienced that sometimes a blue sapphire which is suitable to the nativity, proves very harmful to the native. This is due to some stones, which are born unlucky. Therefore, blue sapphire should only be worn after a trial and got set in the ring only if it does not prove unlucky during the trial period. A trial for about a week should be enough.

By wearing a blve sapphire one gets good servants. The native, will always enjoy happiness, prosperity, name, and fame, advancement in the profession, favours from government. It bestows good health, and success in all ventures. The native will get land, building and properties. It also ensures succ;ess in politics. One could become either a king or a great scholar by wearing blue sapphire.

Note: Blue Sapphire should not be worn by persons born on dates 1, 10, 19,28, 2, 11,20, 29, 3, 12, 21, 30, 4, 13, 22, 31, 9, 18, 27.

8. Gomeda:

Its colour is like red colQured smoke. The Ceylon Gomeda is of honey colour.

Use of Gomeda will bestow good health, win over enemies and bring wealth and prosperity to its owner.

It cures skin diseases, gives knowledge, and intelligence. It promotes good education, and ensures improvement in the profession. J'Jative's business would flourish. The adverse effects caused by evil also vanish. One gets quite active by wearing Gomeda, and gets promotion in the service. It can give unexpected wealth to its wearer" It bestows a very happy life, and the enmity of relatives disappears. Evil spirits go away. It ensures sound sleep and gives peace of mind.

Note: Gomeda should not be worn by persons born on dates 2, 20, 29, 3,12,21,30,7,16,25,8,17,.26,9,18, 27.

9. Cat's Eye:

This is yellowish or blackish in colour. Inside there is a shining band which moves when the stone is turned.

This is a quick-action gem and restores lost wealth. Poverty and d.iseases vanish. It ensures victory over enemies and affords protectiori from enemies. By wearing a Cat's Eye one may be attracted by others. It grants philosophical disposition and activity of the mind. The native gets name, fame and wealth. He becomes calm, and his anger disappears. He receives the help of relatives and friends. Enemies may bow to him. It works successfully in getting back the loan money too. It ensures the welfare of the children. Childless person may be blessed with children. It protects from accident, pimples and skin diseases. It ensures quick marriage.

Note: Cat's Eye should not be worn by persons born on 4, 13, 28, 9, 18, 27

27 Worship Of Stones

Any person who desires to wear a stone whether a precious or a semi-precious one, he should do so on a prescribed day after performing the necessary rituals to the stone. By doing such rituals we are awakening the power of the planet which vests in it. By doing so we can make it give off its vibrations or emanations from its material body in a faster manner. Pooja to Navaratanas has been held in great esteem. Each stone carries in itself the planetary attraction of a particular planet. As a result the rituals should be observed,on the particular planet's day for maximum benefit. It will strengthen its influence. The day and time for each stone is discussed in detail in the following pages. By observing the rituals we can attract the favour and grace of the said planet. Metals also play a very important role in this respect. Metals are also deeply related to the planets and stars, so the correct choice makes a lot of difference. This relation between the metal and gems is enduring and unchangeable.

NO.	PLANETS	METALS
1.	Sun	Copper or Gold
2.	Moon	Silver
3.	Jupiter	Gold
4.	Rahu	Copper or Silver
5.	Mercyry	Silver or Brass
6.	Venus	Silver
7.	Ketu	Silver
8.	Saturn	Silver
9.	Mars	Gold or Copper

After the stone is set in the right combination of gems and metals, it acquires added power through the rituals and subsequent wearing at the appropriate hour.

Method of Pooja for Wearing Gem Stones

1. RUBY: Pooja should be done on any Sunday during "Marshora" between 5am - 6am or 12 Noon and 1pm.

Necessary Pooja Articles

1. Red Silk Cloth, 2. Wheat, 3. Dhoop Sticks, 4. Lamp, 5. 21 Yellow Flowers, and 6. Prasad of Wheat Rawa Upma.

Method

Spread red silk cloth before God and put wheat on it. First wash the ring with the stone set in it. Then apply Sandal, Kumkum on it and place it on the red silk cloth.

Now light the lamps with 5 fates Le., (5 wicks). Burn dhoop stic,do pooja to the ring with yellow flowers reciting Surya Mantra. Offer Upma as Prasad. Now wear the ring. After, the ring is worn, donate jaggery to get maximum benefit.

Surya Mantra

Ashwa Dwajaaya Vidhmahe

Paasha Hasthaaya Dheemahi

Tanno Surya Prachodayath.

Recite this mantra 108 times. (After the Pooja is over divide the yellow flowers into 5 parts, distribute among family members).

2. PEARL: Pooja should be done on Monday during "Chandra Hora" i.e., between 6am - 7am OR 8pm - 9pm.

Necessary Pooja Articles

1. One plate, 2. One kalash, 3. Rice, 4. Curd, 5. Jasmine flowers, 6. Shiv-Parvati Photo.

Method

Pour curd in the kalash and put the Pearl ring in it. Apply sandal, turmeric and kumkum to the kalash. Take a plate and spread rice in it. Now place the kalash on this plate. Close the kalash with another plate and then place Shiv-Parvati photo on it. Perform archana to Parvati Oevi with Jasmine flowers. After the archana is completed, take rice and perform archana to Moon on the rice plate. Offer "Milk Kheer" as Prasad. After wearing the Pearl ring donate milk and mishri.

Moon Mantra

Padma Dwajaaya Vidhmahe

Hema Roopaya Dheemahi

Tanno Soma Prachodayath

Parvati Mantra

Amba SaaTbavi Chandramouli Rabalaam Aparna

Uma Parvati, Kaali, Haimavati, Siva Trinayanaa,

Kaathyaayini Bhairavi.

3. EMERALD: Pooja should be done on Wednesday during the "Budha Hora" i.e., 6am - 7am or 1pm - 2pm

Necessary Pooja Articles

1. One Plate, 2. One Kalash made of Silver or Steel, 3. Rice, 4. Sandal, Kumkum, 5. 5 Betel leaves, 6. Coconut, 7. Green Cloth, 8. Flower Garland, 9. Milk, Sugar, Saffron, Mishri, Elaichi, Eatable Camphor and Rose Water, 10. Any sweet for Prasad.

Method

Take a plate and spread rice over it. Take the kalash and apply Chandan-3 lines each, five times one beside the other in the middle line. Apply Kumkum.

Now, place the kalash over rice plate, pour milk into the kalash mixed with sugar, saffron, mishri, elaichi, eatable camphor and eatable rose water. Now put the Emerald ring in the milk. Keep 5 betel leaves on the kalash. On it keep coconut and apply sandal, kumkum to the coconut.' Put green cloth, flower garland, and perform Lakshmi Mantra 324 times Le., 108 times thrice. Offer sweet as Prasad. After the pooja wear the Emerald Ring. After wearing the Emerald, donate green gram.

Lakshmi Mantra

Maha Devaicha Vidhmahe

Vishnu Patnaicha Dheemahi

Tanno Lakshmi Prachodayath

4. RED CORAL: Pooja should be done on a Tuesday, Thursday and Sunday for 9 days during "Mars Hora" i.e.,

Tuesday	:	6-7am or 1-2pm
Thursday	:	7-8am or 2-3pm
Sunday	:	5-6am or 12-1 pm

Necessary Pooja Articles

1. Red Silk Cloths (two), 2. Copper plate, 3. Tuar Dal 4. Red Flowers, 5. Raagi, 6. Honey

Method

Place red silk cloths before God and spread tuar dal on it. Place the copper plate over the dal. Now place another red silk on it and again spread tuar dal on it. Wash the Coral ring, apply sandal and kumkum.

Take 3, 6 or 9 red flowers, tie them to the ring with the help of a red thread and place the ring on toor dal.

Begin the pooja on one Tuesday and perform continuously for 9 times i.e. on Tuesdays, Thursdays and Sundays. On the 9th day wear the ring after pooja. During the pooja days after the pooja tie the Red Coral in a red silk cloth and keep. Offer honey as Prasad, recite Mars Mantra and· perform pooja with raagi. After pooja is completed donate masoor dal in a red cover.

Mars Mantra

Veera Dwajaaya Vidhmahe

Vigna Hastaaya Dheemahi

Tanno Bhowma Prachodayath

5. DIAMOND: Pooja should be done on a Friday during the "Shukra Hora" i.e., between 6-7am or 1-2pm.

Necessary Pooja Articles

1. One triangular-shaped plate, 2. Blue silk cloth cut into a triangular piece, 3. Rajma, 4. Sandal, Kumkum, 5. 5 types of flowers, 5 types of fruits and 5 types of sweets, 6. 30 betel leaves, 5 blouse pieces, 7. Camphor, 8. 5 packet betel nuts, 9. Haldi pieces.

Method

Take one steel plate of triangular shape and spread Rajma over it. On this put blue silk cloth in triangular shape. On this blue silk cloth keep the Diamond ring after applying sandal and kumkum to it. Now recite Lakshmi Mantra 108 times and after that Shukra Mantra 108 times. Repeat this process for 5 times, Le., 5 times 108 Lakshmi Mantra and 5 times 108 Shukra Mantra. Recite this mantra with 5 types of flowers. After completing the ritual offer 5 types of sweets and 5 types of fruits. Put on the ring. Now distribute betel leaves, haldi pieces, betel nuts, flowers, fruits, sweets and blouse pieces to five ladies and complete the pooja.

Lakshmi Mantra

Maha Devaicha Vidhmahe

Vishnu Patnaicha Dheemahi

Tanno Lakshmi Prachodayath

Shukra Mantra

Ashwa Dwajaaya Vidhmahe,

Dhanur Hasthaaya Dheemahi

Tanno Shukra Prachodayath

6. PUSHYARAGA (Yellow Sapphire): Pooja should be performed on any Thursday during the Hora of Guru Le., between 6-7am or 1-2pm.

Necessary Pooja Articles

1. Yellow coloured cloth (Mango Colour), 2. Bengal Gram (Coated), 3. Sandal, Kumkum, 4. Ketakl Flowers or Marigold flowers, 5. Prasad Le., Kheer Made of Jaggery and Moong Dal.

Method

Spread the yellow cloth before God. Spread Bengal gram on it. On the dal apply sandal, kumkum to the ring and place it on the dal. Take 3 ketaki flowers, or 3 marigold flowers and recite Lalita Sahasnanama. After receiting take the Bengal gram dal, and do Guru Mantra 108 times. After pooja offer kheer made of moong dal and jaggery. After wearing the ring donate Bengal gram.

Guru Manta

Vrishabha Dwajaaya Vidhmahe

Gruni Hasthaaya Dheemahi

Tanno Guruh Prachodayath

7. NEELAM (Blue Sapphire): Pooja should be performed on any Saturday between 6-7am or 1-2pm in the afternoon.

Necessary Pooja Articles

1. Iron or Steel Plate-1, 2. Steel Lamp - 1, 3. Black til, 4. Sandal, Kumkum, 5. Blue flowers, 6. Eight pieces black cloth.

Method

Keep the iron or steel plate. l1ght the steel lamp. Spread til over the plate. Wash the ring, apply sandal and kumkum to' it and place it on the plate. Recite Shani Mantra for 108 times with blue flowers. Offer Prasad of til rice (cooked rice mixed with til). Offer this til rice, black cloth (if it is winter donate black shawl) to eight beggars or poor people along with Rs. 10/- to each one. After pooja is over take the ring to Ayyappa Temple. Perform the Pooja there and put it on.

Shanti Mantra

Kaka Dwajaaya Vidhmahe

Kadga Hasthaaya Dheemahi

Tanno Mandha Prachodayath

8. Gomeda: Pooja should be performed on any Wednesday between 6-7 am or 1-2 pm.

Necessary Pooja Articles

1. One snake idol, 2. Pieces of brown clothes, 3. 1.5 kg. of black urad dal, 4. Sandal, Kumkum, 5. 22 coins of same denomination, 6. 16 flowers, 7. Yellow rice, 8. Prasad made of milk and plantain.

Method

Place the snake idol in front. Spread broWn cloth around it. Spread 1.5kg. black urad -dal on it, and again spread brown cloth over it. Again spread urad dal on it. Wash Gomeda and apply sandal, kumkum to it. Take one flower and tie it with the ring with a red thread. Now place the Gomeda ring over the black urad dal. Newall around it place 22 coins and 16 flowers. Now take yellow rice and perform 108 times Rahu Mantra. After pooja offer plantain mixed with milk. After pooja is over cut the brown cloth into 17 pieces. On every piece place one part of urad dal. Place one coin in it, and tie them into 17 bundles and donate to 17 beggars. Now put the remaining 5 coins in your cash box.

Rahu Mantra

Naaga Dwtijaaya Vidhmahe

Padma Hasthaaya Dheemahi

Tanno Rahu Prachodayath

9. CAT'S EYE: Pooja should be performed on Wednesday between 6-7 am to 1- 2 pm or between 8-9pm.

Necessary Pooja Articles

1. One snake idol, 2. One brass plate, 3. Grey or red cloth, 4. Horse gram,S. Sandal, Kumkum, 6. Curd for offering, 7. One small bowl of sugar.

Method

Place the snake idol ih front. Inside or before it, place the brass plate and spread grey or red cloth over the brass plate. Now wash the Cat's Eye ring, apply sandal and kumkum and place it over the cloth.

Recite Ketu Mantra 108 times. After that offer curd as offering. Wear the ring and donate sugar to somebody along with the bowl.

Ketu Mantra

Ashwa Dwajaaya Vidhmahe

Shoola Hasthaaya Dheemahi

Tanno Ketu Prachodayath

Pooja for Substitute Gems

1. Pooja for Golden Topaz, Garnet, Surya Kantmani, Amber, Peridot etc. Day &: Time: Sunday between 6-7am.

Method

Take a red silk cloth. Spread wheat over it. Wash the ring, apply chandan, kumkum to it and place it on 67 the wheat. Offer agarbathi, camphor and red flowers. Recite the mantra given below 108 times and wear it.

Surya Mantra

Om Gruni Suryaya Namaha

2. Jade, Moon Stone, Day &: Time: Monday or Poomitna 6-7 am.

Method

Take a white silk cloth. Spread rice and sugar ovel it. Wash the ring and apply sandal, kumkum to it. Place it on the rice and sugar mixture. Offer agarbathi, camphor qnd white flowers. Recite the mantra given below 108 times and wear.

Moon Mantra

Om Som Somaya Namaha

3. Yellow Topaz, Amethyst, Yellow Zircon, Yellow Agate, Yellow Tourmaline, ***Day &: Time:*** Thursday Between 6-7am.

Method

Spread Bengal gram on it. Wash the ring and apply sandal and·kumkum to it. Place it on the Bertgal gram. Offer agarbathi, camphor along with yellow flowers and wear.

Guru Mantra

Om Brum Bruhaspataye Namaha.

4. Jaichint, Hessonite Garnet, Day &: Time: Wednesday 6-7am.

Method

Take a brown silk cloth. Place back urad dal on it. Wash the ring and apply sandal and kumkum to it. Place it on the black urad dal and offeragarbathi, carr..phor and rose flowers and recite the mantra given below 108 times and wear.

Rahu Mantra

Om Hraam Rahuve Namaha

5. Aquamarine, Green Onyx, Malachite, Green Zircon, Green Tourmaline, Day &: Time: Wednesday 6-7 am.

Method

Take a green cloth. Spread green moong dal over it. Wash the ring and apply sandal, kumkum and place it over the green moong dal. Offer white flowers, agarbathi and camphor. Recite the Budha Mantra given below 108 times and wear the ring.

Budha Mantra

Om Bhum Budhaaya Namaha

6. White Zircon, White Tourmaline, Spathic, White Opal Turquoise etc., ***Day & Time:*** Friday 6-7 am.

Method

Take a white silk cloth. Spread Rajmah over it. Apply sandal, kumkum to the ring and place it on the white silk. Offer white flowers, agarbathi and camphor. Recite the Mantra given below 108 times and wear the ring.

Shukra Mantra

Om Shum Shukraya Namaha

7. Tiger Eye ***Day &: Time:*** Wednesday 6-7 am.

Method

Take a red silk cloth. Spread horse gram over it. Apply sandal and kurnkurn etc., to ring and place it on the red silk. Offer red flowers, agarbathi and camphor. Recite the Ketu Mantra given below 108 times and wear the ring.

Ketu Mantra

Om Kem Ketave Namaha

8. Blue Zircon, Blue Tourmaline, Neelam, Lolit, Blue Star Ruby, Lapis Lazuli etc., ***Day &: Time:*** Saturday 6-7 am.

Method

Spread a blue silk and place black til on it. Apply chandan and kumkum to the ring and place on the. black til. Offer blue flowers, camphor, agarbathi and wear the ring.

Satrun Mantra

Om Sham Shanaischaraya Namaha

9. Red Cornelian, Red Tourmaline, Fire Opal, Red Jasper etc., ***Day &: Time:*** Tuesday 6-7 am. Method Spread red silk cloth. Place tuar dal on it. Apply chandan and kumkum to the ring after washing the ring. Apply camphor, red flowers and agarbathi. Recite 'the following Mantra 108 times and wear the ririg.

Mars Mantra

Om Aam Angaarakaya Namaha.

28 Gem Stone Selection As Per Zodiac Signs And Stars

You can select your gem according to your st :J or Zodiac sign. The Zodiac or a circle is of 360°. Each division or a house or Rasi (as knownn India) is of 30°. There are 12 divisions of the Zodiac and each has a different ruling planet. The 12 solar months are named after the 12 Zodiac signs. Zodiac Zodiac is divided into 12 equal divisions of 30 degrees. The 30 degrees is again divided for 2¼ stars.

Each star has four pada or parts and 9 such partds are set up for one Rasi or division of Zodiac. Thus each part in 30° is divided by 9 = 3.20 degrees.

The following chart is essential for reference. Your Janma Rasi is in accordance with the position of star pada or part. For example if your star is Krithika 1st part, it is Aries, and if it is Krithika 2nd part, it is Taurus, and so on.

This chart can give you a clear understanding of your Rasi. You would be able to know through your star which Rasi you belong to, and which is your Zodiac sign-and then select your gem accordingly.

1	**Aries or Mesha**		**Degrees**
	Ashwini	1, 2, 3, 4 Parts	
	Bharani	1, 2, 3, 4 Parts	1 to 30
	Krittika	1st Part	
2.	**Taurus or Rishabha**		**Degress**
	Krittika	2, 3, 4 Parts	
	Rohini	1, 2, 3, 4 Parts	31 to 60
	Mrigashira	1, 2 Parts	

3.	**Gemini or Mithuna**		**Degrees**
	Mrigashira	3, 4 Parts	
	Andra	1, 2, 3, 4 Parts	61 to 90
	Punarvasu	1, 2, 3 Parts	
4.	**Cancer or Kataka**		**Degrees**
	Punarvasu	4th Part	
	Pushyami	1, 2, 3, 4 Parts	91 to 120
	Aslesha	1, 2, 3, 4 Parts	
5.	**Leo or Simha**		**Degrees**
	Makha	1, 2, 3, 4 Parts	
	Purva Phalguni	1, 2, 3, 4 Parts	121 to 150
	Uttra Phalguni	1st Part	
6.	**Virgo or Kanya**		**Degrees**
	Uttra Phalguni	2, 3, 4 Parts	
	Hasta	1, 2, 3, 4 Parts	151 to 180
	Chitra	1, 2 Parts	
7.	**Libra or Tula**		**Degrees**
	Chitra	3, 4 Parts	
	Swati	1, 2, 3, 4 Parts	181 to 210
	Vishakha	1, 2, 3 Parts	
8.	**Scorpio or Vrichika**		**Degrees**
	Vishakha	4th Part	
	Anuradha	1, 2, 3, 4 Parts	211-240
	Jyeshta	1, 2, 3, 4 Parts	
9.	**Sagittarius or Dhanur**		**Degrees**
	Moola	1,2, 3, 4 Parts	
	Purvashada	1, 2, 3, 4 Parts	241-270
	Uttarashada	1st Part	

10.	**Capricon or Makara**		**Degrees**
	Uttarashada	2,3, 4 Parts	
	Sharvana	1, 2, 3, 4 Parts	271-300
	Dhanistha	1, 2 Parts	
11.	**Aquarius or Kumbha**		**Degrees**
	Dhanishta	3, 4 Parts	
	Satabhisha	1, 2, 3, 4 Parts	301-330
	Purvabhadra	1, 2, 3 Parts	
12.	**Pisces or Meena**		**Degrees**
	Purvabhadra	4th Part	
	Uttarashadra	1, 2, 3, 4 Parts	331-360
	Revati	1, 2, 3, 4 Parts	

Details of Zodiac Divisions and How to Select the Gem According to your Zodiac Sign.:

1. **Aries or Mesha:** This is the first Zodiac sign. Its ruler is Mars. The gem of Mars is Red Coral. If Mars is afflicted by other planets or debilitated or posited in the negative place in the horoscope, it may give negative effects. If you wear Red Coral, this can protect from the evil effects of Mars. If mars is debilitated or in the enemy house it can lead you to bonded labour. If you wear Red Coral you can get scope for doing independent work or to get promotion in the work. Red Coral will give mental strength, and the glands will work properly.

2. Taurus or Rishabha: This is the second Zodiac sign. This is ruled by Venus. The gem of Venus is Diamond. If Venus is afflicted by other planets, or debilitated, or posited in the enemy house or in negative position in the horoscope Venus may give unfavourable result. However use of Diamond can minimize the evil effects of Venus and produce good effects. This would bring wealth, name, fame and prosperity. Even if Venus is posited in good place in the horoscope, wearing of Diamond will enhance the positive effect.

3. Gemini or Mithun: This is the third Zodiac sign. Its ruler is Mercury. The gem of Mercury is Emerald. If Mercury is afflicted by other planets or debilitated, or posited in the enemy house or in negative position in the horoscope, Mercury will give negative effects. Use of Emerald gives strength to Mercury and wards off its evil-effects. It protects the nervous system, and brings success in education and profession. It also helps in turning other's enmity into friendship.

4. Cancer or Kataka: This is the fourth Zodiac sign. Its ruler is Moon. The gem of Moon is Pearl. If Moon is afflicted, debilitated or posited in the enemy house, or in negative place in the. horoscope, it can result in ill-health to mother, lack of concentration, dull-minded personality, gastric troubles, breathing problems and even asthmatic troubles, These ailments may be cured by. wearing. a Pearl.· Financial success and comfortable life would follow.

5. Leo or Simha: This is the fifth Zodiac sign. Its ruler is Sun. The gem of Sun is Ruby. If Sun is afflicted, or debilitated, or posited in the enemy house, or in negative place in the horoscope, it can cause financial hardship, troubles through officials, or workers, heart diseases, etc. Wearing of Ruby reduces these troubles, and gives success in dealing with the Government officials, fame, social success etc.

6. Virgo or Kanya: This is the sixth Zodiac sign. Its ruler is Mercury. Its gem is Emerald. Wearing of merald will reduce ail stomach disorders, and produce keen knowledge.

7. Libra or Tula: This is the seventh Zodiac sign. The ruler of this sign is Venus."Its gem is Diamond, so if Diamond is worn, it improves the financial position, brings promotion alild abundant wealth.

8. Scorpio or Vrichika: This is the eighth Zodiac sign. The ruler of this sign is Mars. The gem of Mars is Red Coral. By wearing Red Coral one can . achieve success in finance, and get strength of mind and heart.

9. Sagittarius or Dhanur: This is the ninth Zodiac sign., The ruler of this sign is jupiter. The gem of jupiter is Yellow Sapphire, If jupiter is afflicted by other planets, or d,ebilitated, or posited in the enemys house or in negatiye position, it can give unfavourable effects. To ward off these effects one should wear Yellow Sapphire. Through this jupiter gets strength and brings great fortune. The subject would get good name in the society, live comfortably, without any diseases, and get name and fame. Even if jupiter is well posited in the horoscope, wearing of Yellow Sapphire will enhance the good qualities of jupiter.

10. Capricon or Markara: This is the tenth Zodiac sign. Its ruler is Saturn. The gem of Saturn is Blue Sapphire. If Saturn is afflicted or debilitated, or occupying enemy house or posited in negative position in the horoscope, it can produce unfavourable results. Wearing of Blue Sapphire will minimize the evil effects of Saturn, and produce good effects. It helps in doing away with laziness and the subject becomes active mentally and physically. He gets success in the landed and property cases. Unexpected money comes his way. Even if Saturn is posited wellin the horoscope wearing of Blue Sapphire will enhance the good effects of Saturn.

11. Aquarius or Kumbha: This is the eleventh house of Zodiac sign. Its ruler is Saturn. Blue Sapphire is its gem. Wearing of Blue Sapphire brings success and prosperity.

12. Pisces or Meena: This is the twelfth sign of Zodiac. Its ruler is Jupiter. Its gem is Yellow Sapphire. Wearing of Yellow Sapphire brings good fortune to the wearer. A planet if posited in an unfavourablehouse, or debilitated or afflicted. Will lose its strength and produce unfavourable results. Wearing of a particular gem connected to that planet will ward off those bad effects and produce good effects. Even when the planet is posited powerfully in a favourable house, and is a fortune giver in the horoscope, wearing of suitable gem enhances its good qualities and produces more beneficial effects.

29 Gem Stones Selection As Per The Stars

You can choose your suitable gem according to your star also. In all there are 27 stars. Each star is ruled by a specific plant. First you should know your star. Then you should find out which plant is the ruler of that star. Only then you can get that gem of that planet and choose it to wear.

1. Ashwini: The ruler of this star is Ketu, the gem of Ketu is Cat's Eye. If one wears Cat's Eye it would cure different types of diseases and make one healthy and wealthy. He would be attracted by others.

2. Bharani: The ruler of this star is Venus. The gem of Venus is Diamond. Persons born in Bharani star can wear Diamond. Use of Diamond brings material prosperity and happiness.

3. Krittika: The ruler of this star is Sun. The gem of Sun is Ruby. Persons born in Krithika star can wear Ruby. Its use produces good health, success in finance and helps to win over enemies.

4. Rohini: The ruler of this star is moon. The gem of Moon is White Pearl. Persons born under Rohini star can wear Pearl as their lucky gem. It brings position, wealth and success in this life.

5. Mrigashira: The ruler of this star is Mars. The gem of Mars is Coral. So persons born under Mrigashira can wear Coral as their lucky gem. Wearing of Red Coral brings peace of mind, purity of heart, boldness and also helps in controlling anger and wild passions.

6. Andra: The ruler of this star is Rahu. Its gem is Gomeda. So persons born under this star can wear Gomeda for getting fortune. It also bestows intelligence, fame, success in all ventures and peace of mind and self-confidence. The subject would overcome selfishness.

7. Punarvasu: The lord this star is Guru (Jupiter). The gem that should be worn by these persons is Yellow Sapphire (Pukhraj). It brings good luck. It also gives success, fulfillment of desires, healthy body and mind- and makes one rich.

8. Pushyami: The lord of this star is Saturn, and gem is Blue Sapphire. Persons born under Pushya star and wear Blue Sapphirea as their birth stone and get success. It enable them to get money, riches, prosperity, fame, name, house, property, conveyance and luxuries. Moreover it gives them peace of mind and spiritual inclination.

9. Ashlesha: The lord of this star is Mercury. Its gem is Emerald, persons born under this star should wear emerald to get success. By wearing Emerald they can get success in life. They will get good rewards for their talent. It washes away their sins. It can bestow happiness and fortune on them.

10. Makha: The owner of this star is Ketu. Its gem is Cat's Eye. Persons born under Makha should wear Cat's Eye to get success in life as their birth stone. By wearing Cat's Eye they can get name, fame and popularity. It can make them spiritual and guide in that way. It will make them calm and God fearing..

11. Purva Phalguni: Its Lord is Shukra, i.e., Venus. So persons born under this star would wear Diamond to get success. It can give them status, good family life, luxuries and property. They would get multiple profits through business. It will give them charm and beauty.

12. Uttara Phalguni: Its owner is Surya the Sun. The gem for this star is Ruby. Persons born under Uttara Phalguni can wear, Ruby to get luck. It will bestow upon them health, wealth, happiness, good status, success and majestic attraction.

13. Hasta: The owner of this star is Moon. Its gem is White Pearl. So Hasta-born should wear White PI'ar! as their lucky gem. By wearing Pearl they GIIII gel peace of mind, creativity, longevity, good health. success, wealth, riches, name, fame and also popularity.

14. Chitra: The Lord of Chitra is Mars. Its gem is White Peral Chllra-born persons should wear Red Coral to get luck It enables them to get good health, wisdom, spirituality, success, position and also domestic harmony.

15. Swati: The Lor of Swati is Rahu. Its gem is Gomeda. So, Swati born person should wear Gomeda. This can bring them growth in their business or profession. It can ward off any adverse effect of evil eye and black magic. It can make a person active, provide him with high position, name, fame and wealth.

16. Vishakha: Its Lord is Guru Oupiter). Its gem is the Yellow Sapphire. Vishakha-born should wear Yellow Sapphire to get luck. It would bestow royal honour, prestige and health.

17. Anuradha: Its lord is Saturn. Its gem is the Blue Sapphire. So Anuradha-born should wear Blue Sapphire for a happy life. It bestows happiness, prosperity arid also wisdom.

18. Jyeshta: The ruler of this star is Mercury. The gem of Mercury is Emerald. So jyeshta-born persons should wear Emerald as their lucky gem. It would help them to improve their behaviour and conduct. Their anger would cool down, and they will enjoy a happy life.

19. Moola: The ruler of this star is Ketu. The gem of Ketu is Cats Eye, so Moola-born persons should wear Cat's Eye as their luoky gem. It will give them calm and peaceful mind They will receive help from relatives and friends and win over enemies.

20. Purvashada: The ruler of this star is Venus. The gem of Ven\Js' is Diamond, so Purvashada born persons should wear Diamond as their lucky gem. By wearing Dia,mond they would get wealth, comfort, house, vehicle, landed property etc.

21. Uttarashada: The owner of this star is Sun. The gem for sun is Ruby. Hence Uttarashada-born persons should wear Ruby as their lucky gem. It brings wealth, and a prosperous life.

22. Shravana: The owner of this star is Moon. The gem of Moon is Pearl. Persons born under this star should wear White Pearl. They will have a fulfilling life, and their position would improve.

23. Dhanishta: The ruler of this star is Mars. The gem of Mars is Red Coral. So the Dhanishta-born persons should wear Red Coral as their lucky gem. It brings success in all their ventures. They rise in profession. It protects them from dangers and accidents.

24. Shatabhisha: The owner of this star is Rahu. The gem of Rahu is Gomeda. So Satabhisha-born persons should wear Gomeda as their lucky gem. It ensures success in life, good health, and a happy life and strength to win over estranged relatives.

25. Purvabhadra: The owner of this star is jupiter. The gem of jupiter is Yellow Sapphire. So Purvabhadra-born persons should wear Yellow Sapphire as their lucky gem. This would get them hack their lost prosperity, children's welfare, promotion in service, professional success, and happiness.

26. Uttarabhadra: The owner of this star is Saturn. The I'rm of Saturn is Blue Sapphire. So Uttarabhadra born persons should wear Blue Sapphire as their lucky gem. It brings success in the profession or business, acquisition of building and landed property, name, fame and respect in society.

27. Revati: The owner of this star is Mercury. The gem Mercury is Emerald. Hence, Revati-born persons should wear Emerald as their lucky gem. Emerald brings comforts in life. It would also help them to acquire property and success in their profession ..

30 Semi Precious Gem Stones

There are as many semi-precious gem stones as the precious ones. Of all the gems, the following are considered more auspicious and fortunate gems.

These are:

Turquoise, Peridot, Tourmaline, Topaz, Amethyst, Rock Crystal, Moonstone, Garnet, Neeli, Aquamarine, Jade, Blood Stone, Lapis Lazuli, Kidney Stone, Amber, Agate, Jaichint, Green Onyx and Malachite.

1. Turquoise: This is one of the semi-precious stones and it was believed that Venus and Saturn are its rulers. Chemically it is the hydrous phosphate of alumina, coloured by a copper compound an account of its water content. A good turquoise is sky blue in colour.

It emits healing radiation, the shade of greenish-blue. The stone can protect the wearer from injury by falling. It will draw upon itself the evil that threatens its wearer. Unfortunately if any evil is to come to the native, the stone gets broken and the wearer is still protected. It has the power to protect against evils and is a respected. gem stone by muslims. It is a also a lovers' fortunate gem. It keeps a couple intact. It is a fortunate gem for performing quick marriage. It is also lucky for horsemen and riders.

2. Per idot: It is greenish in colour, chemically it is the silicate of magnesium and iron. It is ruled by Sun. Like turquoise it is a fortunate stone for performing quick marriage and protecting the married life. It ensures a happy married life. This gem stone controls the epilepsy disease. It also saves one from poisonous insects. Even if they bite, nothing would happen, and the object would be cured soon.

3. Tourmaline: There are different varieties available in different colours. It is the silicate and borate of alumina, magnesia and iron.

Red, white, green, yellow and blue can be used as sllbstitutes for Ruby, Diamond, Emerald, Yellow Sapphire and Blue Sapphire respectively.

It improves one's knowledge and, promotes good education. It helps the native build good character, respect elders and be responsible.

4. Topaz: This stone stands for friendship and fidelity. It is available in white, pink, black, yellow and smoky colours. Yellow Topaz has magical powers. It is good for health. Its use protects one from a sudden or violent death. It is ruled by Sun. It also helps in toning down negative feelings towards others, and cools down one's temper. It sharpensthe intelligence. It drives away nightmares, and brings sound sleep.

It can guard against injury by fire or accidents. It is a good amulet while travelling and helps one to overcome obstacles on the way. It ensures wealth. It cures eye, liver and kidney disorders and also lungs, nasal disorder, throat diseases and asthma.

5. Amethyst: This is a variety of quartz. Mars, Saturn and Jupiter rule this. It is a light to dark violet coloured gem. It works as a very effective substitute for blue sapphire. It is of iron and manganese oxide. It is an effective antidote against alcohol and saves one from adverse effects of drunkenness. Amethyst controls violent and angry behaviour. It has the power to controll levil thoughts. It protects the person and warns against enemies, sickness and danger. It can ward-off the evil eye, and works as a charm against witchcraft and black magic.

6. Rock Crystal: It is white and clear like ice, with a shining white colour. It prevents bad dreams. It fills women's breasts with milk.. The rays of Sun reflected by crystal have healing power for all eye troubles. These reflected rays should fall only on the body and not in the eyes. It gives good luck, knowledge and wisdom. It has curative power to cure many diseases and even cancer.

7. Moon Stone: It is available in white cloudy colours. Inside the stone there is a glittering band which rolls when the stone is turned. This stone brings good fortune to the native. It has the mystical power of reconciling lovers who had parted in anger. It promises good fortune and success in the affairs of the heart. It can ward off epilepsy, and protect the person against attack by hidden enemies. It cures mentally disturbed persons, and promotes peace of mind. It is a. powerful talisman when there is danger of drowning. This is because of influence of moon upon the tides. It saves from accident in journey. It grants marital happiness. It brings together separated couples.

8. Garnet: Its colour ranges from a fine deep red to a ruby red. Blackish. red garnet is regarded as the finest. Garnet ensures the victory of the wearer in the battle when it is used as a bullet. It brings fortune, health, name, fame and honour, and success in travels. It keeps away bad dreams. It gives energy and strength to body.

It gives success in the court cases. It cures depression and rheumatism. It controls bleeding.

9. Neeli: As its name suggests it is blue in colour. Saturn exercises power through it is the substitute of blue sapphire. It brings success, relief from financial crises and ensures good health to the wearer.

10. Aquamarine: This is of very light greenish white colour. It is ruled by Venus and Mars. It is a fortunate stone for lovers. If one presents this to another it gives them constant mind in love. It protects the sailor in' the sea voyage. It promol education and improves professional prospects,

11. Jade: This is of green colour, but without brilliance or lustre. This is a lucky stone of the Chinese reputed toensure good health and long life. There are two types of Jade: Jadeite and Nephire Jadeite is the silicate of sodium and aluminium. Nephrite is the silicate of calcium and magnesium. It confers long life and a peaceful end. It is a powerful protector against accidents, diseases, witchfraft. It cures epilepsy and all internal complaints. It cures all diseases of kidney and was often referred to as "The Kidney Stone". It strengthens lungs, heart and vocal organs. It is powerful antidote against the poisonous biltes of snakes and other animals. It relieves palpitations of the heart. It brings good luck.

12. Blood stone: This stone is of dark green colour with blood like red spots on it. It cures all kinds of complaints wherein there was loss of blood. It cures bleeding. It protects the wearer from deception, and ensures good health.

13. Lapis Lazuli: This is a stone ruled by Venus and Saturn. It is a soft stone of dark blue colour. This promotes activeness. One get success in cases related to land and properties, chronic diseases, allergies, blood pressure ailments, eye troubles, skin disease may be cured. It brings wealth and property, success in profession and domestic happiness. Women who suffer from stomach pain during menses time should wear this, it would cure their stomach-ache and keep them in good health.

14. Kidney Stone: Light green in colour, it is worn for disorder of kidney. It cures all Kidney disorders and promotes good health.

15. Amber: It protects health and reduces goitre. It relieves stomach pain, and improves liver and kidney functioning. It cures teeth disorders, cold and jaundice. It is also a cough-cure. It is especially favoured for toothache, headache and rheumatic pains.

16. Agate: These are available in red, yellow and white colours. Red is ruled by Mars, yellow by Sun and white by Jupiter.

It ensures happiness; peace of mind. It makes a person brave and courageous. it protects against accidents and troubles through natural calamities. It also brings financial success.

17. Jaichint: It is of orange colour. It is ruled by Rahu. It ensures good health, ,wealth and prosperity: It promotes good sleep. It protects against electrical shock. Diseases like plague, wounds and injuries get cured fast. It cures skin problems.

18. Onyx: It is beautiful green in colour. It protects against evil eye. It is a fortunate stone for lovers. It ensures conjugal happiness, and a good married life with understanding between the couple.

19. Malachite: It is of dark bluish colour with black or green stripes on it. It is ruled by Mercury & Venus. It is helpful in curing common ailments afflicting babies. It promotes good sleep. In love marriage if one presents this to one's partner, the wearer of this gem never changes his or her mind, and becomes constant in mind. It drives away evil spirirs, and wards off evil eye. It cures traubl" related to pancreas, spleen, asthma, menses problems, eye diseases, cholera etc. This is a fortune-giving stone.

31 Abalone Shell

Shells are made up of calcium carbonate and grow in the ocean, forming part of a living ecosystem. Various types of shell have been used as gems for centuries. One of these types include those made up of pearly layers: mother of pearl, abalone and New Zealand paua.

Abalone shell has been used in many cultures as a decorative jewelry and for carvings. A disc of abalone shell is worn on the forehead of Apache girls as they greet the sun in the morning of their initiation into womanhood.

Abalone strengthens the structure of the body and the functions of the heart chakra. Both pearl and abalone shell hold the same divinatory meaning:

- Intimately connected to the sea - represents the tides of emotion
- An easy flow of feelings and sensitivities to others
- Connected to family and particularly motherhood
- Harmony in relationships
- The play and variety of colors represent change as the beauty of existence.

32 Agate Gemstone

Description: A member of the chacedony family. The stone of waxy soft appearance is made up of microscopic crystals of quart laid down in colourful brands.

Enhances: health and longevity confidence/physical & emotional balance/natural vitality & energy/ strength/ courage.

Aids the maintenance or treatment of: regulation of sex drive/ digestive system

Special Features: Agate will enhance the effects of other stones.

Where to wear: Prized as an amulet

Chakra: accordin to colour of the stone

pink/violet-crown
blue- throat
yellow- solar plexus
indigo- brow
green-heart
red- base
Orange-sacral

Zodiac: Gemini/ Leo/ Aries/ Virgo

Birthstone: June

Anniversary: 12th wedding anniversary

Dream: signifies a journey.

Care: Can be washed under lukewarm water with a drop of detergent and water softner- rinse well in clear water as the soapy film can direct from the stone's lustre. Best to dry in the open air.

This is the stone everyone should have for protection. This group of stones are variegated chalcedony. (see also moss agate, eye agate) The agate is one of the oldest stones in recorded history.

Agates attract strength. Agate is a protection from bad dreams. It also protects from stress and energy drains. Agates have been used in jewelry since Biblical Babylonian times. They were used to ward off storms. They were prized gems in antiquity. The agates with banded colors were placed at the head of a sleeper to give rich and varied dreams. Agates have been thought to be good to harden the gums.

Healing properties of agate

Agate is used for stomach upsets. Place the agate on the solar plexus. The agate can't change emotions, but helps to change our level of acceptance of the emotion. Such as when you are very sad the agate will let you know that this will pass and help you get on to another and better day. This is why the Agate is considered so powerful as it gives us the strength to carry on. Carry an agate when you have to make an important decision.

Sources of agate

Probably the most famous place that agate is mined is Idar-Oberstein in Germany where it has been collected since 1548. Other locations to find agate are Uruguay, Brazil, United States, Mexico, Madagascar, Italy, Egypt, India, China, Scotland.

Fire Agate Gemstone

Fire Agate has a deep calming energy that brings security and safety. It is a protection stone with strong grounding powers.

Fire agate links to the fire element and is used as an aid to improve sexual activity, stimulating vitality and opening the base chakra.

Hold a fire agate to inspire inner knowledge to emerge in the resolution of problems. It also helps in overcoming addictions, and other destructive desires.

Healing properties of fire agate

- Heals the stomach, nervous, endocrine systems
- Strengthens night vision
- Reduces hot flashes

Fire agate is said to represent absolute perfection. It instills spiritual fortitude.

Snakeskin Agate Gemstone

This unusual agate resembles the skin of a snake in appearance.

It's energies promote strength in times of excessive activity. It also encourages a pleasant personality by providing inner peace and an appreciation for the simple joy of being alive. As a result, users of snakeskin agate experience increased cheerfulness and self love as well as a renewed love of life.

- Create invisibility by becoming lost in a crowd
- Assist in the reduction of worrying
- Promote self esteem and self-awareness
- Finding lost items

It has been used to initiate the rise of the kundalini (the feminine, dynamic, energetic and creative aspect of the universe from which all form is born).

Healing properties of snakeskin agate

It is used in the treatment of hearing problems and stomach disorders. It has also been used successfully to diminish wrinkles and to soothe the skin.

Tree Agate

Tree Agate is the common name for Dendritic Agate.

The Stone of Plenitude

Place one of these large stones anywhere that you want to encourage abundance and fullness.

Some of the benefits of tree agate include:

- Enhances the health of house plants
- Creates a peaceful environment
- Deepens your connection to the earth

Be patient when using dendritic agate. It works slowly and takes time to be effective. Use it to encourage a more centered viewpoint in life.

Healing with Tree Agate

Healers use tree agate to align and correct anything with branches (such as blood vessels, nerves, skeletal disorders). Place it on a point of pain for relief.

Moss Agate Gemstone

Moss agate is a multi-shade of green that resembles moss or trees from a distance. It is sometimes found with bands of brown agate and when this occurs it is called mocha stone.

Moss agates are considered the most powerful of the agates. It was the agate of warriors. Moss agate is the most powerful of the agates that helps balance emotional energy. It helps the user to let go of anger and bitterness, so the emotions are balanced. When used in jewelry the moss agate is believed to bring the wearer health, friends and riches.

Healing properties of moss agate

Moss Agate strengthens in times of stress.

It is helpful in relieving sensitivities to weather and pollution.

Midwives use it to assist in successful birthing. It is used to speed up recovery, conteract long term illnesses, cleanse the circulatory and elimination systems.

Blue Lace Agate Gemstone

Blue lace agate is one of the rarest and most popular of the agates.

This is a calming, uplifting stone. The blue color strengthens the function of the throat chakra and encourages peace. It can be used wherever there is a build up of painful or irritated energy.

Healing properties of blue lace agate

Wear or carry blue lace agate for peace and happiness. Place it in your hand when you feel the need to de-stress. If you find yourself in stressful situations at work or home, keep some blue lace agate on your desk and simply gaze at it for relief.

In the home, surround blue lace agate stones with light blue candles to calm the atmosphere and reduce family quarrels.

Eye Agate Gemstone

Also known as Botswana Agate, eye agate has been known to ward off the evil eye. This is the gemstone for people who are sensitive and lonely or easily hurt. It will help you have more self-satisfaction and protect you from hurt.

Healing properties of eye agate

Eye Agate or Botswana Agate enhances sexual energy by giving physical stamina.

33

Amazonite Gemstone

Description: A pale bluish-greent for potash feldspar.

Enhances: creativity & communication-good for anyone involved in the arts, clarity of thought, balanced can calm emotions, balanced and aligned physical and mental body, masculine quantities.

Aids the maintenance of treatment of: helps proive relief to those suffering from emotional disturbances.

Where to wear: jewellery around the throat

Chakra: throat

Zodiac: Cancer/Virgo

Care: Can be washed under luke warm water with a drop of detergent and water softener- rinse well in clear water as the soapy film can detract from the stone's lustre. Best to dry in the open air.

This semi-opaque blue-green variety of feldspar is named after the Amazon River.

Amazonite balances feminine and masculine energy. It promotes kindness and practicality. It is an excellent stone for artists and for men.

Pale azure blue amazonite is know as the **lucky "Hope Stone"**. It will be lucky for all your hopes and dreams. Amazonite is blue-green to pale green stone in the feldspar group. It comes mainly from United States and Australia.

Healing properties of amazonite

Amazonite helps balance the emotions and gives physical stamina.

34 Amber And Angelite Gemstone

Description: Amber is the fossilized resin of coniferous trees other containing insect fragments. It ranges min colour from pale yellow to orange and can be opaque or transparent.

Enhances: decision making, memory, luck, strength, enhances body and mind and is harmonious, cheering and soothing.

Aids the maintenance or treatment of: brain, stress, throat ailments (infection/ larynigits) or bronchial disorders (asthma/breathlessness/coughs), general lung care.

Special features: Because it absorbs and turns negative energy into positive energy, it is recommended you cleanse the stone after each use to get rid of any residual negative energy.

Where to wear: in the area from the cheast to the ears but do not cover the throat chakra. Do not wear it for too long at one time.

Chakra: sacral/ solar plexus

Zodiac: Leo/ Virgo/ Capricon

Dream: Signifies a voyage or some kind of movement or change.

Care: Polish regularly with soft cloth and beeswax. It is easily scratched so wrap in soft cloth.

Amber is technically not a gemstone or mineral, but a fossilized sap from prehistoric trees that has aged over the course of millions of years. This Columbian amber is approximately 2 million years old. Baltic amber is considered to be the world's finest. Amber is usually thought of as yellow golden in hue, but amber also can be found in shades of milky white, red-orange, green, black and even (very rarely) violet.

Early physicians prescribed amber for headaches, heart problems, arthritis and a variety of other ailments. In ancient times, amber was carried by travellers for protection. To early Christians, amber signified the presence of the Lord.

Amber energy properties

- Brings a care free, sunny disposition
- Promotes good luck and success
- Dissolves oppositions
- Helps with stomach, spleen and kidney complaints.

Angelite Gemstone

This stone is formed from celestite that has been compressed for many millions of years.

Angelite is a stone of heightened awareness, with special focus on peace and brotherhood. It gives protection in the environment around your body.

- Promotes compassion and understanding
- Helps you to speak the truth when this is difficult
- Alleviates psychological pain
- Enhances astrological understanding
- Increases telepathy
- Facilitates contact with angels

Angelite as a healing stone

Healers use angelite to unblock energy pathways. It can be used for relief from throat inflammations, and to balance the thyroid. Angelite also repairs and soothes tissues and blood vessels. It is very useful for weight control.

35 Amethyst Gemstone

Description: Amethyst is purple to bluish-voilet clear quartz.

Enhances: intution, creativity, memory, motivation, right brain activity, function of pineal and pituitary glands, courage, excellent for meditation soothes mind and focuses attention, serenity.

Aids the maintenance or treatment of: endocrine & immune systems, cleansing organs, curculatory system, headaches.

Where to Wear: Wear it anywhere especially over heart or at throat.

Chakra: brow/ crown.

Zodiac: Pisces/ Sagittarius/ Aries/ Capricon

Birthstone: February

Anniversary: 17th wedding anniversary

Dream: signifies escape from harm.

Care: Can be washed under luke warm water with a drop of detergent and water softener-rinse well in clear water as the soapy film can detract from the stone's lustre. Best to dry in the open air.

Amethyst is a purple coloured stone, which helps the wearer in several ways. Amethyst wards off tendency to switch over from one activity of another, protects the wearer from sudden and unexpected happenings, dangers of witchcraft, devils and evil spirits. Amethyst is also good for financial stability and is good for those, who find it difficult to manage their financial affairs. Amethyst is also good for modern managers, computer scientists and financial experts, particularly those engaged in major or big enterprise. It is good for natives born in the month of Jan or Feb of any year and for piseces (those born between

Feb 21 & March 20). They would acquire magnetic personality and would be able to win over the opposite sex with ease, with the use of this gem.

The Greeks believed that the wearers of this gem would be blessed with happiness and unending love and affection, and enjoy protection from excessive dangers from indulgences like intoxication, temptation to go in for excessive involvements, drugging etc. Scientists, technocrats, mathematicians and research scholars too can use this gem as it would provide them with greater powers for concentration, serousness of purpose, sustained work. Many social reformers who wish to have good public rapport, social welfare like charitable deeds and humanitarian causes have tested this gem with full confidence. Promotions, transfer to their desired levels too can be acquired by the wearer within a few months of the use of this gem. Those dealings with fashion garments, beauty parlours, travel & tourism and show business as also in public relation jobs can hope to achieve instanct success through the use of these gem. Natives with birth number 3 and those with birth numbers 4 and 8 too would find sudden upturn in their financial fortunes as also positions and prestige. If they can acquire and use this gem.

Ametyst is also good for the physical well being of the wearers and is good for those who may wish to give up drinking and wishes to lead a simple and healthy life. This is a recommended Gem stone of the Aquarians. It can also be used with profit and pleasure by Capricornians. Its maximum weight should be 10 carets.

Crystalline quartz in shades of purple, lilac or mauve is called amethyst, a stone traditionally worn to guard against drunkeness and to instill a sober mind. The word amethyst comes from the Greek meaning "without drunkenness" and amethyst is beleived to protect one from poison.

Power Stone

It is used as a dream stone and to help insomnia. Put an amethyst under your pillow to bring about pleasant dreams, or rub it across your forehead to offer relief from a headache.

The amethyst is known as the Bishop's Stone and is still worn by Catholic Bishops. The amethyst symbolizes piety, humility, sincerity and spiritual wisdom. It is thought the amethyst is the perfect stone to symbolize The Age of Aquarius.

Healing properties of Amethyst

Amethyst is a gemstone often worn by healers, as it has the power to focus energy. A healer will usually wear several pieces of jewelry with amethysts set in silver, especially an amethyst necklace. The person to be healed will have an Amethyst to hold while the healing is being done. The healer will place another piece of Amethyst on the area of the body in need of healing, the heart or lungs usually.

Amethyst is used for problems in the blood and in breathing problems. Amethyst crystal clusters are used to keep the air and life force in the home clean and positive.

Amethyst clusters, points or several tumbled Amethysts placed in a window that receives sun most of the day are very beneficial to use in healing and to heal negativity in the home. Place Amethyst clusters, points or several tumbled Amethysts in moonlight and everyone in the home will be feeling calmer. Using an Amethyst as a meditation focus will increase the positive spiritual feelings. Amethyst helps overcome fears and cravings. It also helps relieve headaches.

36 Ametrine Gemstone

Ametrine is a rare and unusual stone which occurs in quartz when amethyst and citrine reside in the same crystal. Because the color zoning effect is natural, no two ametrines will ever be exactly alike.

Ametrine is among an elite group of gems, because as of now there is just one source of this treasure in the world. You should add an ametrine to your collection now, since its future availability is uncertain at best.

Healing properties of Ametrine

Ametrine is very helpful in getting rid of depression. This leads to inner peace and tranquility.

Many believe that it contains the powers of amethyst and citrine in one stone, making it a very powerful money stone as well as an excellent via to higher psychic awareness and spiritual enlightenment.

Apatite

Apatite is most often seen in blue, but also can be found in pink, yellow, green (from Spain called asparagus stone) and a rare variety of violet.

Apatite is an inspirational stone. It develops psychic abilities and spiritual attunement. Use it to aid communication and self-expression.

- Encourages extroversion
- Dissolves alienation
- Draw negativity from oneself
- Stimulates creativity and intellect
- Clears confusion.

Healing properties of Apatite

Apatite heals bones, aids absorption of calcium, helps cartilage, bones, teeth and motor skills. Relieves arthritis, joint problems. Overcomes hypertension.

37 Aquamarine Gemstone

Description: A clear blue-green form of Beryl

Enhances: intution, creativity, memory, motivation, right brain activity, function of pineal and pituitary glands, courage, excellent for meditation-soothes mind and focuses attentio, serenity.

Aids the maintenance or treatment of: endocrine & immune systems, cleansing organs, circulatory system, handaches

Where to wear: wear it anywhere especially over heart or at throat.

Chakra: brow/ crown

Zodiac: Pisces/ Sagittarius/ Aries/ Capricon

Birthstone: February

Anniversary: 17th wedding anniversary

Dream: signifies escape from harm

Care: Can be washed under luke warm water with a drop of detergent and water softener- rinse well in clear water as the soapy film can detract from the stone's lustre. Best to dry in the open air.

Aquamarine appears in various shades of blue. It goes well for tender skin and can be worn with considerable success for girls in the age group of 15-18. Aquamarine is also a recommended stone for devout Hindus and others who may be inclined towards humanitarian and spiritual aspects of life and want to probe deeper into the mysteries of nature. It is an ideal gem for those born on 3rd. 12th, 21st, or 30th of a month (birth number 3) or for Pisces or for those in whose cases Jupiter is well placed in the ascendant in their natal charts. It is also a recommended stone for Leo. It should be worn by those who are interested in outing or entertainments or those involved in public relations jobs. It would also reduce tensions stresses in personal relationships, strengther emotional ties and can protect the wearers in cases where others may exploits or play on their kind heartedness or gnerosity.

Aquamarine is highly recommended for those engaged in teaching and research, banking, medicine, humanitarin causes, travel and tourism, film industry, sailors and navigators and those interested to benefit from overseas connections. Aquamarine signifies courage and determination and bestows investigative powers as well as marital happiness. Aquamarine is best for those who have ego problems and cannot control their temper.

This is the stone to help you **be in touch with your spiritual being.** This stone is used in deep meditations.

Aquamarine is a blue-green stone that comes from Colombia and Brazil. It has been called "Water of the Sea", because of its color. The aquamarine is the stone of sailors, believing it would be protection for them on water. Folklore says the aquamarine will protect against gossip. It is also said the aquamarine will pick up spirits. It is an excellent stone to use for mediating.

Aquamarine is most powerful as a meditation stone, as it brings a great peace and serenity. Some people can meditate on an Aquamarine to receive the wisdom to see truth, but this is a very advanced meditation.

Healing properties of Aquamarine

Aquamarine is associated with the thymus gland. It is very soothing worn as a necklace. It will help reduce fluid retention. It has been used to calm the nerves.

The Romans used the aquamarine for diseases of the stomach, and believed it could cure liver and throat troubles.

38 Alexandrite Gemstone

The magic of changing colours

The most sensational feature about this stone, however, is its surprising ability to change its colour. Green or bluish-green in daylight, alexandrite turns a soft shade of red, purplish-red or raspberry red in incandescent light. This unique optical characteristic makes it one of the most valuable gemstones of all, especially in fine qualities.

Alexandrite is very scarce: this is due to its chemical composition. It is basically a chrysoberyl, a mineral consisting of colourless or yellow transparent chrysoberyl, chrysoberyl cat's eye and colour-changing alexandrite (also in cat's eye varieties). It differs from other chrysoberyls in that it not only contains iron and titanium, but also chromium as a major impurity. And it is this very element which accounts for the spectacular colour change. Rarely, vanadium may also play a part. According to CIBJO nomenclature, only chrysoberyls displaying a distinct change of colour may be termed alexandrite.

Alexandrites are also recovered from sources in Sri Lanka, but the hue of these stones compares less than favourably with that of the Uralian alexandrites. They appear green in daylight and a brownish red in artificial light. The Tunduru area in southern Tanzania has also produced some outstanding specimens since the mid-1990's. Alexandrites are also found in India, Burma, Madagascar and Zimbabwe. Although this stone is still considered a rarity, specialised gemstone dealers do stock it, especially since improved trade relationships between Russia and the rest of the world have ensured a better supply of Russian alexandrites to the market.

39 Aventurine Gemstone

Description: A variety of quartz found in shades of blue, brown, red and green with greene being the most commonly used form. Mica flakes give it an iridescent sheen. (There

Enhances: intution, creativity, memory, motivation, right brain activity, function of pineal and pituitary glands, courage, excellent for meditation-soothes mind and focuses attentio, serenity.

Aids the maintenance or treatment of: endocrine & immune systems, cleansing organs, circulatory system, handaches

Where to wear: wear it anywhere especially over heart or at throat.

Chakra: brow/ crown

Zodiac: Pisces/ Sagittarius/ Aries/ Capricon

Birthstone: February

Anniversary: 17th wedding anniversary

Dream: signifies escape from harm

Care: Can be washed under luke warm water with a drop of detergent and water softener- rinse well in clear water as the soapy film can detract from the stone's lustre. Best to dry in the open air

You should never buy a lottery ticket without an aventurine in your left pocket. Lady Luck will be in your left pocket. This is the stone of opportunity. Aventurine is known as the stone of chance or luck. If you gamble or play the lotto, keep this stone in your left pocket.

Aventurine is mainly quartz, a quartzite, usually containing mica. The color of aventurine is green ranging from a pale green to deep forest green. Aventurine is mainly from India.

Aventurine is the stone of luck and chance. It is said to increase perception and creative insight.

Healing properties of Aventurine

It is used to aid nearsightedness. Aventurine has a stabilizing effect on the emotions. It is excellent for teenagers.

40 Aragonite Gemstone

Aragonite varies in color and can be white, gray, colorless, yellow, pale green, violet, or brown. Aragonite is also the primary mineral that makes up the organic compound commonly known as

Aragonite is a grounding stone. It is often used to center and ground physical energies and is very useful during stressful times. Aragonite stabilizes the base chakra, and strenghtne your connection with the earth.

Healing properties of aragonite

- warms the extremities, bring energy through the entire body
- aids calcium absorption
- stops night twitches and muscle spasms.

Sources of Aragonite

Locations for occurrence are found in Spain, Mexico, Morocco, New Mexico, and Arizona. It was first discovered in Aragon province, Spain where its name was derived.

Aventurine is the stone of luck and chance. It is said to increase perception and creative insight.

Healing properties of Aventurine

It is used to aid nearsightedness. Aventurine has a stabilizing effect on the emotions. It is excellent for teenagers.

41 Azurite Gemstone

Description : A deep blue copper-based stone often growing near or with malachite.

Enhances: sleep, meditation, psychic abilities, clarity of mind, creativity of mind, creativity, mental health stability, energy flow, abortion of oxygen.

Aids the maintenance or treatment of: thyroid gland, heart, circulatory system, pineal and pituitary glands, brain, skeletal system, tissue regeneration.

Where to wear: earlobes or around the throat

Chakra: brow/ throat

Zodiac: Sagittarius

Care: Can be washed under luke warm water- safest to avoid detergent- rinse well in clear water and dry in the open air

The dark brilliance of azurite speeds the vibration of energy toward the spiritual realm.

Azurite has a transformative quality that stimulates an increase in communication skills, intuition, creativity and inspiration.

Place azurite on the third eye chakra during meditation. It will open up your inner sight. It is an excellent stone for students who are studying for exams. It helps open the mind and make it more receptive to retaining information.

Healing properties of azurite

- Liver stimulant
- Aids detoxification
- Stimulates brain and nerve activity
- Encourages growth by stimulating the activity of the thyroid gland.

Sources of Azurite

Azurite is found in copper mining areas such as Australia, Chile, the former USSR, Africa, China.

42 Bloodstone Gemstone

Description: A green form of chalcedony (a member of the quartz family) flecked with red spots of jasper. Also called heliotrope.

Enhances: Physical and mental vitality, mental clarity and balance, physical strength, wisdom, courage, moderation of aggression and violence.

Aids the maintenance or treatment of: bloodstream- strengthen/ oxygenate/ circulation, respiratory tract, varicose veins, depression & psychosomatic illness, cleansing organs, iron deficiencies.

Where to Wear: earlobes and around the throat

Chakra: base / heart **Zodiac:** All signs

Birthstone: March **Dream:** signifies distressing news

Care: Can be washed under luke warm water with a drop of detergent and water softener- rinse well in clear water as the soapy film can detract from the stone's luster. Best to dry in the open air.

Bloodstone (also called heliotrope) is green with distinctive red spots that resemble blood, giving this stone its name. The bloodstone was used to stop bleeding especially nosebleeds.

Healing properties of bloodstone

The bloodstone is used for circulation of all energy in the body and helps to remove energy blocks. Bloodstone is used in the alignment of all the centers of the body. A healer must do this alignment while the patient lies on his stomach. It also aids in the circulation of blood. It is good to have several pieces of Bloodstone in the home to increase the flow of life energy.

Sources of bloodstone

Locations where bloodstone can be found include India, Brazil, China, Australia, and the United States.

43

Clear Optical Calcite (Iceland Spar) Gemstone

Calcite is a powerful amplifier and cleanser of various types of energies. This transparent crystal can be found in a variety of colors including clear, green, pink, orange and blue.

Clear (Iceland Spar) variety displays an optical illusion called double refraction - when you look through the crystal, it splits the light rays in twc, producing a double image. For this reason, it is often used in magic rituals to double the power of a magic spell.

Optical calcite amplifies images and helps you to see double meanings hidden in communication.

Healing properties of Clear Calcite

- Reduces tension
- Heals the eyes
- Relief for migraine headaches

Sources of Clear Calcite

Calcite is found in a wide variety of locations throughout the world.

Pink Calcite (Mangano Calcite) gemstone

Calcite is a powerful amplifier and cleanser of various types of energies. This transparent crystal can be found in a variety of colors including clear, green, pink, orange and blue.

Pink Calcite is a heart crystal with strong forgiveness properties. Use it to release fear and grief that has trapped your love energy from a past incident. It is an excellent remedy to increase self-worth. It has a soft loving energy that will dissolve resistance.

Healing properties of Pink Calcite

- Heals nervous conditions
- Alleviates anxiety, grief, trauma and tension
- Prevents nightmares

Sources of Pink Calcite

Calcite is found in a wide variety of locations throughout the world.

Blue Calcite gemstone

Calcite is a powerful amplifier and cleanser of various types of energies. This transparent crystal can be found in a variety of colors including clear, green, pink, orange and blue.

Blue Calcite

- Brings about stability
- Calming stone
- Stimulates trust in oneself
- Enhances memory
- Effective against laziness

Healing properties of Blue Calcite

Blue calcite can be used as a healing stone when worn or placed between blue or purple candles. It is often used in purification rituals.

Some of its healing uses are:

- stimulates metabolism
- strengthens the immune system
- stabilizes the rhythm of the heart
- lowers blood pressure
- dissolves pain

Sources of Blue Calcite

Calcite is found in a wide variety of locations throughout the world.

Green Calcite gemstone

Calcite is a powerful amplifier and cleanser of various types of energies. This transparent crystal can be found in a variety of colors including clear, green, pink, orange and blue.

Draw money and prosperity by burning green candles placed around green calcite for a short while each morning.

Green Calcite draws money and prosperity to your doorstep.

Healing properties of Green Calcite

Green calcite can assist in dissolving old rigid belief systems, restoring balance to your mind. It aids any transition from a stagnant to a positive environment. It is also used to stimulate the immune system and absorb negative energy (such as arthritis and bacterial infections). Crystal Healers use it with bone adjustments, and constrictions of the ligaments and muscles.

Sources of Green Calcite

Calcite is found in a wide variety of locations throughout the world.

44 Carnelian Gemstone

Description: A type of chalcedony (a member of the quartz family) which is translucent or clear and red to orange to dark brown in colour.

Enhances: motivation, clarity of mind, meditation, concentration, memory, self confidence, vocal expression, peace and harmony, courage.

Aids the maintenance or treatment of: lower back problems, lungs, blood, reproductive organs, cleansing organs, tissue regeneration, depression.

Special Features: Works well with amethyst to develop higher mental awareness.

Where to wear: short pendant or buckle

Chakra: solar plexus / sacral / heart

Zodiac : Aries / Leo / Virgo / Capricon **Birthstone :** July

Dream: signifies impending misforture

Care: Can be washed under luke warm water with a drop of detergent and water softener- rinse well in clear water as the soapy film can detract from the stone's lustre. Best to dry in the open air.

Carnelian (also sometimes referred to as cornelian) is found primarily in India, as well as various sites in South America. It is a variety of chalcedony. The most favorable pieces are a deep red to red-orange hue. Carnelian has a long and storied past, and was once considered strictly the property of the noble class. People holding a high social status were often buried with this gem stone.

Want more pep in your life? Keep a carnelian with you and feel the energy flow to you. Carnelian is used for these benefits:

- gives energy
- protects from bad vibrations
- guards against poverty
- helps give a sense of humor
- calms the temper.

Healing properties of Carnelian

Carnelian is an energy booster. It helps the insecure person to find strength within them so they can come into their own. It is said to increase the appetite.

45 Chrysanthemum Gemstone

Chrysanthemum stone is named for its unique patterns embedded in the stone that resemble flowering chrysanthemums.

It is a stone that awakens your true purpose in life and lends the support and courage necessary to follow your dreams. This stone brings unexpected opportunities (luck) once you have stepped on a chosen path.

Chrysanthemum stone contains an energy that forges through obstacles to joy, love and abundance in your life.

It creates a sense of balance between physical and spiritual and encourages love and joy. The flowering pattern represents the burst of energy that is love, joy and abundance.

This unique stone makes a wonderful gift for anyone starting out on a new path (such as an infant or someone making a career change) or between lovers embarking on a new life together. It helps one to start and to continue.

Meditate with chrysanthemum to assist in overcoming fear and obstacles in order to achieve abundance, contentment and joy!

Diamond : Not Necessarily Colorless

However, diamond is the modern birthstone for April, so we would like to take this opportunity to say a few words about fancy colored diamonds, which are more to our taste than the colorless type: more rare, more valuable, and way more colorful (although the colors can tend to be a little pale).

Fancy colored diamonds are not a mass-market product that are advertised everywhere and sold by the numbers. They have more personality than that. Fancy colored diamonds are almost as much fun as colored gemstones! Like colored gemstones, each one is different. They come in fabulously expensive pale pinks and blues, pale to bright yellows, oranges, greens, and all those brown colors that are now being called names like cognac and champagne. So, buy a diamond instead of a colored gemstone if you must, but at least consider a fancy colored diamond which will give your jewelry more character, more individuality, more color!

46 Aquamarine Gemstone

From the light blue of the sky to the deep blue of the sea, aquamarines shine over an extraordinarily beautiful range of mainly light blue colours. Aquamarine is a fascinatingly beautiful gemstone. Women the world over love it for its fine blue shades which can complement almost any skin or eye colour, and creative gemstone designers are inspired by it as they are by hardly any other gem, which enables them to create new artistic cuts again and again.

Its light blue arouses feelings of sympathy, trust, harmony and friendship. Good feelings. Feelings which are based on mutuality and which prove their worth in lasting relationships. The blue of aquamarine is a divine, eternal colour, because it is the colour of the sky. However, aquamarine blue is also the colour of water with its life-giving force. And aquamarine really does seem to have captured the lucid blue of the oceans. No wonder, when you consider that according to the saga it originated in the treasure chest of fabulous mermaids, and has, since ancient times, been regarded as the sailors' lucky stone. Its name is derived from the Latin aqua (water) and mare (sea). It is said that its strengths are developed to their best advantage when it is placed in water which is bathed in sunlight. However, it is surely better still to wear aquamarine, since according to the old traditions this promises a happy marriage and is said to bring the woman who wears it joy and wealth into the bargain. An ideal gem, not only for loving and married couples.

47 Fire Opal Gemstone

Fire opals are unique in the lush world of the opals. They were already admired as symbols of the most fervent love in ancient times, in India and in the ancient Persian kingdom, and among the peoples of Central America and the Amerindians. It was believed that a gem that bubbled over with vivacity to such an extent as the fire opal could only have been created in the waters of paradise. The Mayas and Aztecs loved this gemstone and liked to used it in mosaics and for ritualistic purposes. They called it quetzalitzlipyollitli, the 'stone of the bird of paradise'. Yet one day, the gemstone knowledge of Mexico's natives, which had been handed down from generation to generation, somehow sank into oblivion for a long time .

A powerful gemstone with a vivacious colour

The fiery, warm glow of the fire opal beguiles jewel enthusiasts the world over. This radiant orange simply cannot be overlooked! The fire opal, which, like the other opals, consists of silicic acid with a relatively high water content, was named for its colour. The colour itself comes from fine traces of iron oxide. With a hardness of between 6 and 6_ on the Mohs Scale, however, the fire opal is among the somewhat sensitive gemstones which require a protective setting, especially when worn as a ring stone.

Not all fire opals are the same. We differentiate between the common fire opals, which, depending on their quality, are either faceted or cut into cabochons, and the especially valuable ones, which, in addition to their vivacious colour, also have the gaudy play of colour typical of opals. But with or without play of colour, the fire opal plays its part as a top quality gemstone to perfection.

Even those who prefer not to subscribe to the energies in gemstones and the forces which emanate from them will undoubtedly get a feeling of warmth and well-being when they look at a fire opal. In gemstone therapy, opals are generally regarded as gems which people choose intuitively when they are working on a particular aspect of their personality. Seen like this, the fire opal is a good means of helping to make feelings flow and resolve blockages. Connoisseurs say that fire opals bestow courage, stamina, will-power and energy on the wearer. Thanks to their force they disperse old, long outdated ways of thinking and make room for new ones. The warm, fiery orange-red has a positive effect on the psyche and conveys a profound sensation of warmth, peace and harmony. The fire opal is the lucky stone of those born under the sign Aries.

A gemstone for people with a positive approach to life

Play of colour, body colour and transparency are the three criteria which determine the price of a fire opal. The more transparency and 'fire' it has, and the more intense the deep red of its body colour, the more valuable it will be. The rarest, and thus the most highly esteemed, is the intense red-orange fire opal from Mexico with its strong play of colour. A higher value is placed on fine cabochons with the much loved typical play of colour of the opals than on good, faceted fire opals. These gems, which glow from orange to red, are treasures which appeal most of all to active people with a positive approach to life. Their warm, fiery colour gives us vigour, fills us with the joys of life and opens our senses to the beauty of Nature. After all, fire opals are themselves a piece of Nature in its most beautiful form.

48 Tourmaline Gemstone

Description: These elongated, heavily streaked, brittle crystals come in five main colour types - Verdelite (green), Indicolite (blue), Rubellite (pink), Achroite (colourless) and Schorl (black)

Enhances: communication, co-operation, tranquillity, disperses negativity, sleep, strength of mind and body, inspiration, self confidence, clearing of chakras, memory, creativity

Aids the maintenance or treatment of: balance of endocrine, lymphatic and digestive systems, fear, negativity, nervousness

Special Features: It is best not to wear black or green tourmaline for long periods of time. Wear next to the skin for best effect. Works well with gold.

Where to Wear: according to chakra colour

Chakra/Zodiac: Black - base Green - heart / solar Scorpio / Capricorn / Pisces Blue - crown/ throat Red/Pink - heart / base I Leo / Libra / Cancer / Aries / Sagittarius Pink/Green - heart / base Colourless - all chakra/zodiac

Birthstone: October

Dream: signifies an accident

Care: As for quartz.

Tourmalines are precious stones displaying a unique splendour of colours. According to an ancient Egyptian legend this is the result of the fact that on the long way from the Earth's heart up towards the sun, Tourmaline travelled along a rainbow. And on its way it collected all the colours of the rainbow. This is why nowadays it is called the "Rainbow gemstone".

49 Chrysocolla Gemstone

Description: A blue-green stone resembling turquoise with a high copper content.

Enhances: metabolism, creative expression, wisdom, discretion, Communication, emotional balance- alleviate fear / stress/ guilt.

Aids the maintenance or treatment of: digestive problems, absorption of Vitamin C and assimilation or iron, lungs, circulation, heartache, bone strength, arthritis and rheumatism, hair health.

Special Features: Often known as the feminine stone it is excellent for female health problems.

Where to Wear: as a pendant and around the throat.

Chakra: heart / throat

Zodiac: Taurus / Virgo/ Gemini/ Leo

Birthstone: September

Care: Can be washed in luke warm water- safest to avoid detergent- rinse well in clear water. Best to dry in the open air.

Chrysocolla is a very beautiful stone with many beneficial energies.

It is known as a healing stone among Native American Indian cultures where it was used for strengthening the body's resistance and bringing about calm feelings where there is upset.

Chrysocolla is a stone of peace, increased wisdom, discretion.

It promotes level headedness, encouraging clarity of thought and a neutral, cool attitude during turbulence. It can be used to decrease nervousness and irritability.

Healing properties of Chrysocolla

Chrysocolla can be placed directly on the affected body part. Laying it on the forehead as a 'third eye' offers spiritual benefit.

- Help with infections (especially the throat area)
- Used by healers to detoxify the liver, lower blood pressure
- Has a cooling effect for fever reduction
- Can assist in speeding up recovery from burns
- Alleviates cramps

Sources of Chrysocolla

It is found in copper mining areas, particularly Chile, the former USSR, and Zaire.

Dolomite meaning

Dolomite was discovered in 1791 by Dolomieu while travelling in the Alps.

Dolomite encourages self-realization. It also fortifies a sense of tradition and helps us acclimate to new communities.

Healing properties of Dolomite

Dolomite stimulates the metabolism of calcium and magnesium and keeps a balance between the two. It is used by healers to stabilize health, especially blood, the heart, and circulation. It dissolves cramps.

Dolomite can be worn or laid on the skin. The strongest effect is achieved by spending time in a stone circle of dolomite.

50 Fluorite Gemstone

Description: Also called fluorspar. A very common mineral that occurs mostly in cubes, it is translucent and comes in shades of white, brown, blue, purple, red, yellow as well as colourless.

Enhances: Concentration, intuitive powers, analytical abilities, spiritual awareness.

Aids for maintenance or treatment of: mental disorders, stress, blood vessels, spleen, arthritis, rheumatism, lower back pain, teeth, bones.

Special Features: Use in conjunction with calcite and pyrite.

Where to wear: earlobes **Chakra:** according to colour

crown – purple brow – blue **heart** – green

Zodiac: Pisces

Care: As it can be easily scratched, fluorite needs to be protected if set into jewellery by using high setting.

Formerly called fluorspar, fluorite has a wide range of colors including yellow, blue, pink purple and green. It is an interesting and beautiful stone because often more than one color occurs in a single stone. The ancient Egyptians used flourite to carve statues and scarabs, the Chinese have used it in carvings for over 300 years. In the 18th century, fluorite was powdered in water to relieve the symptoms of kidney disease.

Fluorite is said to absorb and neutralize negative vibrations. It makes one more receptive to the vibrations of other stones. Fluorite should be kept in every room of the home. Fluorite is known as the "Genius Stone".

- increases concentration
- helps in decision-making

Healing properties of Fluorite

Fluorite may be used with other stones. It helps to open the way for the power of other stones to be effective. It can be used as a meditation stone to help energize the body and raise the power of concentration.

Healers use it to help with ulcers as well as the respiratory tract by stimulating cell regeneration in these areas. It fortifies bones, improves arthritic or other joint ailments. It can be laid directly on the body.

Sources of Fluorite

Locations where fluorite is found include Canada, USA, South Africa, Thailand, Peru, Mexico, China, Poland, Hungary, Czechoslovakia, Norway, England, and Germany.

Andalusite : Cognac Cocktail

Andalusite is named after Andalusia, the province of Spain where it was first discovered.

When they succeed, andalusite looks unlike any other gemstones, with patterns of color dancing around the facets. The best color play is seen in fancy shapes, particularly rectangular cushion shapes: in round cuts, the colors blend together.

Andalusite is mined in Brazil and Sri Lanka.

In the past andalusite was sometimes called "poor man's alexandrite" because it offers color play at a low price. But andalusite really doesn't look much like alexandrite, which changes from green to red in different light. It is not really a color change stone at all because the colors are there at the same time.

That should not diminish its appeal, especially for those who like earth tones. Andalusite offers a lot of impact for a relatively low price. Because of its color and its durability, it is especially appropriate for mens jewelry.

51 Citrine : Mellow Yellow

Description: variety of quartz found in a pale golden yellow shade as well darker shades. It is actually Amethyst that has been heated in the crust of the earth. A lot of citrine available for purchase is actually amethyst artificially reheated by man.

Enhances: self- confidence, creativity, healing energy, self esteem, motivation, inner calm, security, release of negative feelings/ anxieties/ fears.

Aids to maintenance or treatment of: cleansing organs- detox blood, digestive organs, heart, digestion, tissue regeneration, circulation, mental disorders.

Special Features: Worn at night it can help prevent nightmares.

Where to Wear: anywhere

Chakra: Solar plexus/ sacral / crown

Zodiac: Leo / Virgo / Scorpio

Care: Can be washed under luke warm water with a drop of detergent and water softener- rinse well in clear water as the soapy film can detract from the stone's lustre. Best to dry in the open air.

Citrine is one of the most affordable gemstones, thanks to the durability and availability of this golden quartz. Named from the French name for lemon,"citron," many citrines have a juicy lemon color.

Citrine includes yellow to gold to orange brown shades of transparent quartz. Sunny and affordable, citrine can brighten almost any jewelry style, blending especially well with the yellow gleam of polished gold.

In ancient times, citrine was carried as a protection against snake venom and evil thoughts.

Most citrine is mined in Brazil. Supply of citrine is good from the Brazilian state of Rio Grande do Sul, particularly from the Serra mine, which is producing 300 kilos a month of hammered goods. The Iraâ mine produces an additional 100 kilos a month of hammered goods.

Sometimes you will hear citrine referred to as topaz quartz, which is incorrect. This name was used in the past in reference to the color, which is sometimes similar to the color of topaz. Since topaz is a separate mineral, this type of name can be confusing and should not be used. However, citrine is considered an alternative to topaz as the birthstone for November.

Since most citrine on the market started its life as amethyst which was heated to turn its color to gold, citrine jewelry, as well as amethyst jewelry, should be kept away from prolonged exposure to strong light or heat. With this precaution, citrine jewelry will last for many generations.

Ametrine: Spinning Purple into Gold

Do you love both the purple of amethyst and the sunny gold of citrine? Are you a rabid Minnesota Vikings fan? I have the perfect gem for you! Sometimes amethyst and citrine colors are found in the same crystal of quartz. These bicolor yellow and purple quartz gemstones are called ametrine.

With ametrine, you can have both gem colors for the price of one! Ametrine is especially inexpensive when you consider that it comes from only one mine in the world.

52 Garnet Gemstone

Description: A group of silicon, aluminum and oxygen based stones that can be grouped as one for holistic purposes. Pyrope (dark red), Almandine (reddish brown), Spessartite (yellow to brownish red), Grossular (green), Andradite (green to black), Uvarovite (deep green), Rhodolite (pinkish-red).

Enhances: strength, endurance, self esteem, imagination, creativity, courage, confidence, meditation, patience, compassion.

Aids the maintenance or treatment of: tonic for whole system, circulation, mental depression, calcification (arthritis etc.), thyroid, toxicity, pituitary gland, nightmares.

Special Features: Best if cut or shaped.

Where to Wear: earlobes / over the heart

Chakra: base / heart

Zodiac: Aquarius / Aries / Leo / Scorpio / Capricorn

Birthstone: January

Dream: signifies solving of a mystery

Care: Can be washed under luke war water with a drop of detergent and water softener- rinse well in clear water as the soapy film can detract from the stone's lustre. Best to dray in the open air.

Garnets - aren't these the wonderfully deep red gemstones which are often found in antique jewellery? Well, this is only the partial truth, as a warm and deep red is indeed the most frequently occurring colour for Garnets. But unfortunately only few people know that the realm of Garnets holds many more bright and beautiful colours.

53 Red Garnet

Healing properties of Garnet

Garnet comes in many colors, but now we will speak only about red Garnet. The Garnet is associated with the thyroid and spleen. It helps cleanse and purify both when held over the area. The Garnet is usually held in the hand or placed on top of the head when searching or meditating on past lives. Information that is beneficial and helpful will usually be released for the searcher.

The Garnet is a stone of purity and truth as well as a symbol of love and compassion. The information released in a search may be painful, but it will always be what the searcher needs. The Garnet will help everyone's security level and spiritual awareness. It can help increase the sex drive.

Red Garnet can also be used with considerable advantage by heart patients or those under stress or strain. Red Garnet relieves tensions and gives relaxation. It is also a recommended stone or ladies having birth number 4 or 8 those ladies, who suffer from body pains, headaches etc. It shoudl be wornaround neck. It is also effective in case of blood pressure. It is associated with gentleness, affectionate nature, kind heartedness, sincerity, frankness, charity, constancey and truthfulness.

Red Garnet can also be used by politicians, surgeons, defence personal and those in the services with advantage. Red garnet is also good for those having their birth numbers 1 or 9. It can also be used by those natives having birth 2 but occupying number 1 position in large organisations. The use of this stone under proper guidence can ensure them long, frutiful and uninterrupted careers.

54 Rubellite Tourmaline Gemstone

Tourmalines Rubellite is an outstandingly beautiful gemstone from the colourful Tourmaline family. Its colours sparkle in the most beautiful shades from red to pink.

Tourmalines are closely related gemstones which are supplied by Nature in many different colours. The trade generally uses no separate denominations for the individual varieties, but rather adds the colour to the name Tourmaline, thus referring to red, green, yellow or blue Tourmalines. But there are exceptions to this rule: this applies especially to the red and pink stones.

Red and pink Tourmalines come in many different shades from palest shell-pink via bold pink to a deep ruby red. But only a selected few of these are called "Rubellite". The name is derived from the Latin term "rubellus" which means "reddish". Bur Rubellites are not simply red or pink Tourmalines. This exceptionally beautiful gemstone shows a decisive characteristic: its steady colour in daylight and artificial light. In fact, many gemstones change their colour depending on the source of light. A Rubellite never changes colour: it shines as brilliantly and clearly in daylight as in artificial light. In contrast to this, the colour of most other pink and red Tourmalines shows a more or less noticeable brownish hue in artificial light.

While it is essential that the cutter bears in mind the different distribution of colour, Rubellites are cut in various ways. The majority of the stones are found in Brazil, Madagascar, Mozambique, Nigeria and Pakistan. Some beautiful pink Rubellites have been discovered in a gemstone mine in the USA.

55 Green And Pink Tourmaline

Tourmaline is a virtually unique colour miracle: this gemstone exists in red and green, blue and yellow, and even in colourless and black respectively. Often there are even two or more colours displayed in one and the same Tourmaline crystal. Highly coveted rarities are colour changing Tourmalines or chattoyant ones. However, the classical colour for Tourmaline is green. And if you ask gemstone dealers for Tourmaline, the green variety will almost inevitably be the first one to come to their minds.

Nevertheless, even the green Tourmalines come in a wide range of shades. Some are very light, others are so dark that the green colour is only discernible when light is shone through the stone. There are green Tourmalines in fine leek-green shades, but there are also intensely coloured yellow-green, olive-green and brownish-green stones. And especially the colour range from blue-green to darkest bottle-green is covered spectacularly by wonderful Tourmalines, for these colours are the best for these stones. They are rare and highly coveted. Tourmaline is loved as a perfect jewellery stone by many women, but it has also come to be preferred nowadays by quite a few men.

Pink Tourmaline Gemstone

Tourmaline comes in various colours like blue green, red, reddish brown, pink etc. It is a recommended stone for those wishing to improve their financial position and status. It is also good for wishing to have a greater concentrations in studies and those appearing in competitive examinations. It is also good for those who wish to be slim and trim. It can be used by all for good luck and prosperity as it has no evil effects. It can forewarn the wearer of any mishaps. Green colour gem is beneficial for businessmen and those who are engulfed with problems of one kind or the other may use the gem in Pink Red. It is very useful for politicians, leaders, writers, etc. It should be worn in silver only.

56 Red Goldstone Gemstone

Description: A soft mineral ranging from deep gold yellow with a metallic lustre that never tarnishes.

Enhances: balance of emotional extremes, confidence, appreciation of others, balances energy fields, mental stimulation, regeneration physical / mental / spiritual planes.

Aids the maintenance or treatment of: circulation, detox blood, nervous system, digestion, hormonal and chemical imbalances, tissue regeneration.

Special Features: Work well with all crystals and gems.

Where to wear: wear anywhere on the body

Chakra: sacral / heart / crown

Anniversary: 50th wedding anniversary

Care: Gold in both its natural and manufactured state is a very soft material and care needs to be taken that it is not subjected to undue pressure.

Goldstone is a man made gemstone that has been around since the European Rennaissance. Early monks working at a glass factory near Venice, Italy were practicing alchemy when molten copper accidentally tipped into a molten glass container.This crystallized into thousands of tiny crystals and formed a melt with golden light sparkles. This is how the first goldstone came about. Though it is not technically a gemstone, it is often referred to as one.

Red goldstone is associated with vitality and energy. Goldstone is an energy stone.

57 Haematite Gemstone

Description: An iron rich ore that is metallic grey to earthy red in colour.

Enhances: energy, vitality, mental capabilities, self esteem, courage, optimism

Aids the maintenance or treatment of : blood- circulation/ oxygenation / cleansing, stress, heart, spleen, breathing disorders, rapid pulse, headache, fatigue, backache

Special Features: An excellent all round healer that draw illness from the body.

Where to Wear: at the base of the spine

Chakra: solar plexus / base / heart

Zodiac: Capricorn

Care: Haematite will usually lose its polish after about six month's wear- there is little that can be done.

Hematite is used to improve relationships. If you need your personal relationship to be better, carry a hematite with you always.

The name comes from the Greek word for blood. It has been used as an amulet against bleeding, and so is known as the "blood stone". When arranged like the petals of a flower, it is referred to as the "iron rose". Native American folklore states that war paint made from hematite will make one invincible in battle. People in the eighteenth and nineteenth centuries wore hematite jewelry during mourning.

Scientists of the Mars Exploration Rover Project believe that deposits of hematite on Mars may help prove whether large amounts of liquid water ever flowed on Mars' surface. They say that where water was, life may have had a chance to thrive as well.

Hematite is good for increasing intuition. In jewelry it is best in a ring worn on the left hand.

Healing properties of Hematite

Hematite stimulates iron absorption in the small intestine, which in turn improves oxygen supply to the body. It can be in direct contact with the skin, but results in inflammation for some people, so test it carefully on yourself before use.

Sources of Hematite

Brazil is the most important source of hematite. Other sources include: China, Canada, England, and Germany.

HerkimerDiamond Gemstone

The Herkimer diamond is double pointed Quartz Crystal that has already been faceted by nature.

- very strong power
- used in out of the body travel
- assists in communicating with other plains and kingdoms

Herkimer Diamonds help connect the astral plane with the earth plane.

Healing properties of Herkimer Diamond

Herkimer Diamond is double terminated crystal (there is a point at each end of the crystal). It is water clear and different from Quartz. It is a very powerful balancer of the body and emotions and should be used carefully. Double terminated equals super power.

Sources of Herkimer Diamond

The Herkimer comes from only one place - Herkimer, New York, in the United States. The bedrock in which the crystals are found began forming approximately half a billion years ago in a shallow Cambrian Sea that lapped against the southern shores of the ancestral Adirondack Mountains (near the town of Herkimer, New York).

58 African Jade And Howlite Gemstone

Description: This term actually refers two different minerals of similar appearance and composition – nephrite (spinach / yellow green and uniform in colour)

Jadeite (broad colour range, can be spotted or striped and is harder than nephrite)

Enhances: peace, serenity, wisdom, memory, emotional balance, clarity, removal of negative energy, benevolence, expressive ability.

Aids the maintenance or treatment of: cleansing system and organs, toxin removal, heart, high blood pressure urinary ailments, fluid, digestion, depression.

Special features: Use the chakras and associated colour as a guide to the best colour for certain organs or ailments.

Where to Wear: anywhere – not for long periods of time except for green and lavender.

Chakra: all chakras depending on colour

Zodiac: all signs especially Virgo / Taurus.

Care: Be gentle with these stones- they can break if knocked

Jade is an ancient stone that has historically been **used to attract love**. Carved into a butterfly, in China it is a powerful symbol used to draw love.

Jade can be used to bring money into your life. Create a positive attitude towards money and visualize yourself using money creatively and productively while holding the stone in your power hand. When making an important business decision, use the prosperous energies of jade by holding it while contemplating your course of action. Jade strengthens your mental faculties and assists in clear reasoning.

Jade is also a protective stone, guarding against accidents and misfortune. Place a piece of jade between two purple candles and let the candles burn for a short while. Then carry the jade with you as a protection amulet.

Healing properties of Jade

The soothing green color of jade makes it a wonderful healing stone. It helps the body in self-healing while working through underlying, non-physical reasons for a precipitation for disease. It is particularly helpful for kidney, heart and stomach complaints.

HOWLITE GEMSTONE

Howlite can be found in green, white and blue. It is a super-calming stone and many people use it to releive stress of all kinds. It makes an excellent antidote to insomnia due to an overactive mind.

Focusing on a piece of howlite can assist in journeying outside the body and gaining insight from past lives. Placed on the third eye, it opens memories of previous times and lifetimes.

Howlite teaches patience

Place a howlite stone in your pocket to absorb your own anger - or another's anger that is directed toward you. It helps to overcome critical or selfish behaviour.

Healing properties of howlite

- Relieves insomnia
- Balances calcium levels
- Strengthens teeth and bones

59 Jasper Gemstone

Description: An opaque form of chalcedony (member of the quartz family) and is actually a mix of chalcedony (member of the quartz family) and is actually a mix of chalcedony, quartz and opal. Colours include red, green, grey, ochre, brown.

Enhances: mental processes, endurance, balance on all levels

brown- stability

red- assertiveness, sensitivity

yellow- mental clarity, channel positive energy

Aids the maintenance or treatment of: green- upper torso ailments, cleansing organs, digestive system, immunity, depression.

Red- circulatory system, blood cleansing orgns

Yellow- endocrine, cleansing organs, intestine

Special features: Works over long periods of time and works well with opal.

Where to Wear: anywhere

Chakra: brown- sacral　　red – base

Yellow – solar plexus　　green – heart

Zodiac: Virgo

Dream: Signifies love returned

Care: Can be washed under luke warm water with a drop of detergent and water softener- rinse well in clear water and dry in the air.

Beautiful multi-colored jasper eggs. Jasper is one of the oldest known gemstones. It is mentioned in the Bible several times. Jasper is a strong securing gemstone. It is a stability gemstone. It is a powerful protection against things that are not good for you and it eases emotional stresses, making it a wonderful gemstone to have in your home.

Jasper gives one the courage to speak out and have personal independence. It also protects from fears in the night. Red jasper is thought to help balance the energy in the body. All jaspers help balance the emotional energy in the body.

Healing properties of Jasper

Jasper comes in many colors. All colors of Jasper will help balance the vibrations of the body. Jasper is slow to show a change to the person, but is such a basic "good" stone that one should always have it on hand.

Leopard Skin Jasper Gemstone

There are many types of jasper; it is one of the oldest known gemstones. It is mentioned in the Bible several times. All jaspers are strong securing, stability stones. It is a powerful protection against things that are not good for you and it eases emotional stresses, making it a wonderful gemstone to have in your home.

Leopard skin jasper is associated with shaman travel and spiritual discovery. It helps you to connect with your spiritual animal totem and traverse between the worlds in order to learn the lessons of your personal totem.

Healing properties of Jasper

Jasper comes in many colors. All colors of Jasper will help balance the vibrations of the body. Jasper is slow to show a change to the person, but is such a basic "good" stone that one should always have it on hand. Leopard skin jasper is said to assist in self-healing.

Red Jasper Gemstone

A strong protection gemstone, red jasper is known to protect against hazards of the night. Red jasper is very lucky for actors. Jasper is one of the oldest known gemstones. It is mentioned in the Bible several times. Jasper is a strong securing gemstone. It is a stability gemstone. It is a powerful protection against things that are not good for you and it eases emotional stresses, making it a wonderful gemstone to have in your home.

Jasper gives one the courage to speak out and have personal independence. It also protects from fears in the night. Red jasper is thought to help balance the energy in the body. All jaspers help balance the emotional energy in the body.

Healing properties of Jasper

Jasper comes in many colors. All colors of Jasper will help balance the vibrations of the body. Jasper is slow to show a change to the person, but is such a basic "good" stone that one should always have it on hand.

Red Jasper helps with the sense of smell. It also promotes physical energy.

Rainbow Jasper Gemstone

A strong protection gemstone, red jasper is known to protect against hazards of the night. Red jasper is very lucky for actors. Jasper is one of the oldest known gemstones. Jasper is a strong securing gemstone. It is a stability gemstone. It is a powerful protection against things that are not good for you and it eases emotional stresses, making it a wonderful gemstone to have in your home.

Jasper gives one the courage to speak out and have personal independence. It also protects from fears in the night. Red jasper is thought to help balance the energy in the body. All jaspers help balance the emotional energy in the body.

Healing properties of Jasper

Jasper comes in many colors. All colors of Jasper will help balance the vibrations of the body. Jasper is slow to show a change to the person, but is such a basic "good" stone that one should always have it on hand. Rainbow jasper is said to ease emotional stress. Carry rainbow jasper and feel relaxed and secure.

Putting a rainbow Jasper in a glass of water for 3 days and then drinking the water is considered a tonic for good health.

Yellow Jasper Gemstone

A strong protection gemstone, jasper sustains and supports during times of stress. Jasper is one of the oldest known gemstones. It is mentioned in the Bible several times. Jasper is a strong securing gemstone. It is a stability gemstone. It is a powerful protection against things that are not good for you and it eases emotional stresses, making it a wonderful gemstone to have in your home.

Yellow Jasper offers protection during spiritual work and physical travel. It channels positive energy. It stimulates the solar plexus chakra.

Healing properties of Jasper

Jasper comes in many colors. All colors of Jasper will help balance the vibrations of the body. Jasper is slow to show a change to the person, but is such a basic "good" stone that one should always have it on hand.

Yellow Jasper releases toxins and helps with digestion in the stomach.

60 Kunzite Gemstone

Description: These striated columnar or tabular crystals are purplish-pink colour with a high lithium content. It is actually a form of Spodumene,.

Enhances: self love, calmness, self esteem, balance on all levels, tenderness.

Aids the maintenance or treatment of: rejuvenate the skin and tissue, heart, tension, circulatory system, lungs, psychiatric disorders

Special Features: Considered a feminine stone. The best colour are the lilac shaded pieces.

Where to wear: pendant over the heart **Chakra:** heart

Zodiac: Taurus/ Libra / Scorpio

Care: Can be washed under luke warm water with a drop of detergent and water softener- rinse well in clear water as the soapy film can detract from the stone's lustre. Best to dry in the open.

Kunzite was discovered at the Pala Chief Mine near San Diego, California and named after gemologist GF Kunz, who first described it after the turn of the twentieth century. Kunzite is an unusual, and rare, stone.

Wear kunzite to be **blessed with good fortune**. Its soft pastel colors **symbolize purity**. It can also be a **sign of new life** and is sometimes regarded as a symbol for pregnancy.

Kunzite is a calming, relaxation stone:

- Releases tension
- Promotes a peaceful disposition
- Emits exceptionally tranquil vibrations

Healing properties of Kunzite

Gaze at or hold a kunzite to release daily stress, smooth out knotted muscles, calm nerves, anger or fear.

Sources of Kunzite

Kunzite is mined in US, Brazil, Madagascar, Myanmar and Afghanistan.

61 Labradorite Gemstone

Description: Also known as Spectrolite, this stone is a form of feldspar. It is to all appearances a dull grey stone until it is titled. At certain angles, it comes alive with iridescent coloured spots and is considered be a mystical stone.

Enhances: higher consciousness, patience, balance and protection of aura, telepathy, medication

Aids the maintenance or treatment of: lymphatic system, nervous system, liver

Special features: Considered a mystical stone, it is recommended for times of trouble.

Where to Wear: earlobes, around throat, pendant.

Chakra: crown/ throat/ heart

Zodiac: Aquarius/ Pisces/ Sagittarius / Capricorn

Care: Can be washed under luke warm water with a drop of detergent and water with a drop of detergent and water softener- rinse well in clear water as the soapy film can detract from the stone's lustre. Best to dry in the open air.

Labradorite is a power stone, allowing you to see through illusions and determine the actual form of your dreams and goals. It is excellent for strengthening intuitions.

Use labradorite to:

- Stimulate imagination
- Develop enthusiasm and thus, new ideas
- To see more clearly in meditation

Sources of Labradorite

Labradorite was first found in 1770 on the Labrador Peninsula in Canada. It is also found in Norway, and the former USSR. There is a blue semi-transparent variety called spectrolite that is only found in Finland.

62 Lapis Lazuli Gemstone

Description: Lapis Lazuli is actually a rock made up of a number of other minerals including laurite, pyrites, sodalite, calcite, micas and more. It is the content of lazurite that determines its quality while the content of lazurite that determines its quality while the golden pyrite grains also increase its value.

Enhances: creative expression, thought amplification, psychic awareness, courage, intellect, enlightenment, balance on all levels.

Aids the maintenance or treatment of: respiratory system, immunity, depression, thyroid, nervousness, grief / melancholy, eyesight, stomach pain, brain

Special Features: This stone should not be worn for long periods of time or even all day.

Where to wear: as close to the throat as possible- above mid stomach to draw energy upwards.

Chakra: brow/ heart **Zodiac:** Libra / Taurus / Aquarius\ Sagittarius

Dream: signifies a love that is faithful.

Care: Best to have it professionally cleaned from time to time.

Lapis Lazuli is a soft gem stone of blue colour. It should have some natural little gold spots. Lapis Lazuli represents tenderness, sympathy and love. Its use is recommended for those, who are born under the solar sign Taurus. Lapis Lazuli is particularly favourable for ladies engaged in music dance, drama. Lapis Lazuli is also helpful to those who believe in subtle values. Persons using this gem will be known by their powers of love and affection and can generally win over others through the powers of love. They would find that they can transmit love to others with ease and confidence. They would also love peace and harmony and acquire an optimistic outlook.

Healing properties of Lapis Lazuli

Lapis Lazuli is used with other stones when parts of the body need to be purified and cleansed and should be only used by a healer. Lapis Lazuli has high intensity and can open many of the charka centers. This must be done only with love in the heart and comprehension in the mind and wisdom in soul.

Zircon

Description: These brittle, usually four-sided crystals come in a variety of colours - clear (white), yellow (Jargon), orange (Jacinth), Red (Hyacinth) and Brown (Malacon) and green. Some zircons contain radioactive elements.

Enhances: mind, sleep, balance emotions, self esteem, aura, mental processes (clear), alertness (yellow), energy in times of physical stress (red), grounding and centring (brown)

Aids the maintenance or treatment of: pituitary and pineal glands, spleen skin disorders, cleansing organs, allergies, depression (yellow), fear and jealousy (orange), pain (red)

Where to Wear: anywhere

Chakra: all chakras

Zodiac: Leo / Virgo / Sagittarius **Birthstone:** December

Care: Can be washed under luke warm water with a drop of detergent and water softener - rinse well in clear water as the soapy film can detract from the stone's lustre. Ultrasonic cleaning can lead to loss of colour as well as damage the stone as it is quite brittle.

Hindu poets tell of the Kalpa Tree, the ultimate gift to the gods, which was a glowing tree covered with gemstone fruit with leaves of zircon. Zircon has long had a supporting role to more well-known gemstones, often stepping in as an understudy when they were unavailable.

In the middle ages, zircon was said to aid sleep, bring prosperity, and promote honor and wisdom in its owner. The name probably comes from the Persian word zargun which means "gold-colored," although zircon comes in a wide range of different colors.

Natural zircon today suffers for the similarity of its name to cubic zirconia, the laboratory-grown diamond imitation. Some don't realize that there is a beautiful natural gemstone called zircon.

Zircon occurs in a wide range of colors but for many years, the most popular was the colorless variety which looks more like diamond than any other natural stone due to its brilliance and dispersion.

Today the most popular color is blue zircon. Most blue zircon, which is considered an alternate birthstone for December, is a pastel blue, but some exceptional gems have a bright blue color. Zircon is also available in green, dark red, yellow, brown, and orange.

Zircon is mined in Cambodia, Sri Lanka, Thailand, Myanmar, Australia, and other countries.

Zircon is one of the heaviest gemstones, which means that it will look smaller than other varieties of the same weight. Zircon jewelry should be stored carefully because although zircon is relatively hard, it can abrade and facets can chip. Dealers often wrap zircons in individual twists of paper so that they will not knock against each other in a parcel.

The wide variety of colors of zircon, its rarity, and its relatively low cost make it a popular collector's stone. Collectors enjoy the search for all possible colors and variations.

Iolite: Gem of the Vikings

The Viking mariners used thin pieces of iolite as the world's first polarizing filter. Looking through an iolite lens, they could determine the exact position of the sun, and navigate safely to the new world and back.

The name iolite comes from the Greek ios, which means violet. Iolite is usually a purplish blue when cut properly, with a softness to the color that can be quite attractive.

Iolite is readily available and surprisingly affordable. The better and richer the blue, the better. It is mined in India, Sri Lanka, Mozambique, Zimbabwe, and Brazil. The Vikings probably mined iolite from deposits in Norway and Greenland.

Iolite is relatively hard but should be protected from blows. With its attractive color and reasonable price, it may become a jewelry staple in the future.

Spinel: Collector Favorite

Spinel is the great imposter of gemstone history: many famous rubies in crown jewels around the world are actually spinel. The most famous is the Black Prince's Ruby, a magnificent 170-carat red spinel that currently addorns the Imperial State Crown in the British Crown Jewels after a long history: Henry V even wore it on his battle helmet! The Timur Ruby, a 352-carat red spinel now owned by Queen Elizabeth, has the names of some of the Mughal emperors who previously owned it engraved on its face, an undeniable pedigree!

Now treasured for its own sake, spinel is a favorite of gem dealers and gem collectors due to its brilliance, hardness and wide range of spectacular colors. In addition to beautiful rich reds, spinel can be found in a range of beautiful pastel shades of pink and purple. Of particular interest is a vivid hot pink with a tinge of orange that is mined in Burma that is one of the most spectacular gemstone colors in any gem species. Spinel also comes in beautiful blues which are sometimes called cobalt spinel, but these are very very rare.

Because spinels made in a laboratory are often used for imitation birthstone rings, many people think "synthetic" when they hear the name "spinel." They have often never even seen the real thing.

In fact, the main thing holding back greater recognition for spinel is rarity. Fine spinels are now more rare than the rubies they used to imitate. Strangely, they are also more affordable: in the gem world, too rare can be a drawback because so few people even get a chance to grow to love these gem varieties.

In addition to Burma, now known as Myanmar, spinel is mined in Sri Lanka, Tanzania, and Tadjikstan, part of the former Soviet Union.

Spinel is a durable gemstone that is perfect for all jewelry uses. It is most often faceted in oval, round, or cushion shapes and is not currently found in calibrated sizes due to its rarity.

Chrysoberyl

Like the eye of a sleek feline predator, the chrysoberyl cat's eye winks at the astonished observer – a real miracle of Nature! That's why only this attractive gemstone has the right to the short, fitting name of "cat's eye". This gem is really something special with its narrow, bright band of light on a shimmering golden background, which seems to glide magically across the surface when the stone is moved.

(For your information: cat's eye effects can also occur in other gemstones, but these always have to be referred to more precisely by adding the name of the gemstone concerned: e.g. quartz cat's eye.)

Often, the name chrysoberyl is spoken in the same breath as that of the beryl group, the most well known representatives of which include the emerald and the aquamarine. The name 'chrysoberyl' comes from the Greek and means 'gold-coloured beryl'. In spite of its name however, it is not actually a beryl at all. Together with alexandrite, chrysoberyl forms an independent gemstone, in which the former, which appears to change its colour, is regarded as the most attractive representative, though in fact it is quite definitely the chrysoberyl cat's eye which is entitled to stake that claim.

From a mineralogical point of view, chrysoberyls are aluminium oxide containing beryllium, and thus actually have little in common with the beryls, which belong to the silicate family. Indeed, with their excellent hardness of 8_ on the Mohs Scale, they are clearly superior to the beryls. The popular chrysoberyls come in many nuances between lemon and greenish yellow, and in honey colours and shades from mint green to brownish green, and are mostly found in the gemstone deposits of Brazil, Sri Lanka or East Africa.

Protection and positive energy

Since ancient times, chrysoberyl has been regarded as a gemstone which protects its wearer and keeps disaster at bay. The cat's eye most of all is seen as a particularly effective protective stone and talisman. On account of its golden tones, chrysoberyl is often also associated with wealth – and this idea is certainly not without foundation, since in its most beautiful form as a high-quality cat's eye it is up among the gemstones of the luxury class.

Discipline and self-control are the qualities mainly associated with chrysoberyl in modern gemstone therapy. Chrysoberyls are said to promote concentration and the ability to learn, and to enable the wearer to think clearly and far-sightedly. Thanks to the secret power of the chrysoberyl, negative thoughts are said to be transformed into positive energy. And these positive qualities are said to be even more marked with a chrysoberyl cat's eye. However, chrysoberyl is also regarded as a gemstone which promotes tolerance and harmony, and it is one of the lucky stones for those born under the sign of Leo.

The magical eye of the cat

Chrysoberyl cat's eyes are genuine rarities which are found only in a few deposits in the world, together with other varieties of chrysoberyl. One can hardly imagine that a gemstone could wink like the eye of a cat in such a remarkably genuine way. Is it magic, or Nature? And apart from that, what is it that causes this irresistibly beautiful show of light?

64 Quartz: Common Chameleon

If you gaze deep inside a crystal ball, you will see a versatile gemstone, one of the most popular gems on earth. Beautiful quartz, the "rock crystal" used in ancient times to make crystal balls and bowls, is today more often seen set in gold jewelry. Despite the popularity of quartz gems like amethyst, citrine, ametrine, rose quartz, onyx, agates, chrysoprase, rutilated quartz, and other quartz gemstone varieties, many people in the jewelry industry take quartz for granted because of its affordable price.

Throughout history, quartz has been the common chameleon of gemstones, standing in for more expensive gemstones ranging from diamond to jade. But the incredible variety of quartz is now beginning to be appreciated for its own sake.

Purple to violet amethyst and yellow to orange citrine are jewelry staples that continue to increase in popularity. Ametrine combines the appeal of both amethyst and citrine as well as both the purple and yellow in one bicolored gemstone. Different colors and types of chalcedony, from agate to chrysoprase, have grown in popularity with the growing appreciation for carved gemstones and art cutting and carving. And unusual quartz specialties like drusy quartz, with its surface covered by tiny sparking crystals, and rutilated quartz, which has a landscape of shining gold needles inside, are adding variety and nature's artistry to unusual one-of-a-kind jewelry.

Rose quartz

The pale pink color of quartz, which can range from transparent to translucent, is known as rose quartz. The color is a very pale and delicate powder pink. Transparent rose quartz is very rare and is usually so pale that it does not show very much color except in large sizes. The translucent quality of rose quartz is much more available and is used for beads, cabochons, carvings, and architectural purposes.

Smoky quartz

Smoky quartz is a brown transparent quartz that is sometimes used for unusual faceted cuts. The commercial market is limited due to the limited demand for brown gemstones. This variety was sometimes known as smoky topaz in the past, which is incorrect and misleading, since the mineral variety is quartz, not topaz.

Tiger's Eye

Tiger's Eye quartz contains brown iron which produces its golden-yellow color. Cabochon cut stones of this variety show the chatoyancy (small ray of light on the surface) that resembles the feline eye of a tiger. The most important deposit is in South Africa, though Tiger's eye is also found in Western Australia, Burma (Myanmar), India and the U.S. (California).

Rock crystal

The transparent colorless variety of quartz is still known as rock crystal. Long ago, people believed that rock crystal was a compact form of ice: crystallos actually means "frozen." The best rock crystal has the clarity and shimmer of water. Although colorless quartz is relatively common, large flawless specimens are not, which is why crystal balls these days are made of glass, not quartz. Rock crystal has often been used in jewelry, particularly carved pieces. Many stunning Art Deco jewelry designs featured the black and white quartz combination of rock crystal and onyx. Colorless quartz crystals have also become popular in jewelry due to the popularity of legends about the powers of quartz crystals. Many people believe that wearing quartz crystals benefits a person's health and spiritual well being.

65 Malachite Gemstone

Description: A copper carbonate ore with layers or brands ranging in colour from the palest green to the deepest black green.

Enhances: expression, patience, physical endurance, inner peace, intuitiveness, emotional clarity, sleep.

Aids the maintenance or treatment of: stress, heart, circulatory system, pineal and pituitary glands, teeth, cramp prevention, rheumatism, arthritis, tissue regeneration, menstrual regularity, mental disorders.

Special Features: Works well with azurite. Because of its high copper content, it is poisonous and should not be take internally. It is said to break if danger imminent.

Where to Wear: ring on left hand

Chakra: heart/ solar plexus

Zodiac: Capricorn / scorpio

Birthstone: July

Dream: signifies impending misfortune

Care: Can be washed under luke warm water- safest to avoid detergent- rinse well in clear water. Best to dry in the open air.

Malachite is believed to be a strong protector of children. It is said to protect the wearer from accidents and protects travelers. Malachite has been used to aid success in business and protect against undesirable business associations. It is a stone of balance in relationships.Malachite is always green, usually in banded tones varying from very dark green to a mellow green. Most malachite comes from Zaire, Chile and Australia.Ancient Egyptians, Greeks and Romans used malachite for jewelry and ground it to use as eye shadow. It is used in amulets to protect against the evil eye. In the Middle Ages it was used to protect children from witches and other dangers.

To help get rid of nightmares, keep a piece of Malachite in your bedroom.

66 Moonstone Gemstone

Description: A member of the feldspar family, moonstones can be colourness, grey to bluish white and transparent, opalescent or milky.

Enhances: calm response to overreaction, feminine nature, sensitivity, intuition, psychic abilities, attraction of friendship and loyalty, sleep, confidence, balanced emotions, balance of female / male energies.

Aids the maintenance or treatment of: pituitary gland, digestive system, cleansing organs, reproductive organs, obesity, water retention, lymphatic system, females- hormonal and menstrual problems.

Special features: Said to be more magically potent during the waxing moon.

Where to Wear: as a ring.

Chakra: heart

Zodiac: Libra/ Cancer / Scorpio/ Pisces

Birthstone: June

Anniversary: 13th wedding anniversary

Dream: signifies impending danger

Care: Can be washed under luke warm water with a drop of detergent and water softener- rinse well in clear water. Best to dry in the open air.

Passionate love that will fly you to the moon

It is said if you give your lover a moonstone necklace when the moon is full you will **always have passion** with each other. Moonstone is a highly valued gemstone for these reasons:

- Brings good fortune
- Assists in foretelling the future

- Enhances intuition
- Promotes inspiration
- Brings success in love as well as business matters
- Offers protection on land and at sea

The moonstone is associated with the moon and was the stone of the goddess Diana. **The most powerful time to use the moonstone is in a full moon.**

It has been worn as an amulet to bring good emotions to the wearer, while protecting those of a sensitive nature. **It can reunite lovers who have quarreled.** Moonstone is also considered a good luck stone.

Moonstone is a very personal stone. It is a reflection of the person who owns it. It does not add or detract, only shows how it is. This is why the moonstone is said to perceive that which "is". Moonstone is an **excellent stone to use in meditation to understand oneself.** Placing it in the moonlight of a moon reaching its fullness, not a full or waning moon, can revitalize it. This is a particularly good gemstone for women. It is a good stone for young women or teenagers.

Healing properties of Moonstone

Moonstone stimulates the functioning of the pineal gland and balances internal hormone cycles with nature's rhythms. Moonstone is a stone of inner growth and strength. Though often considered to be a woman's stone, it can be beneficial to men in opening the emotional self.

Sources of moonstone

There are two moonstones. Adularia moonstone is an almost transparent pale gray or silvery white or blue shimmer. It is mainly found in Sri Lanka, Burma, India and Madagascar. Albite moonstone is in the feldspar group. It is semitransparent with a pale, shimmering reflection. It may be a little dull. It comes mainly from Canada.

67 Onyx Gemstone

Description: Onyx is actually a variety of agate and is a black and white banded version of the stone.

Enhances: strength - mental and physical, concentration, devotion, balance of yin and yang energies and male/female polarities, emotional health, self control, happiness

Aids the maintenance or treatment of: teeth, bones, bone marrow, stress, depression, balance of sexual impulses

Special Features: Because it helps improve concentration, it is often found in rosaries.

Where to Wear: on left side of body or over solar plexus

Chakra: root

Zodiac: Capricorn

Dream: signifies marital happiness

Care: Can be washed under luke warm water with a drop of detergent and water softener - rinse well in clear water as the soapy film can detract from the stone's lustre. Best to dry in the open air.

Onyx is known to separate. It can help release negative emotions such as sorrow and grief. It is used to end unhappy or bothersome relationships.

Onyx guards against negativity

Onyx jewelry is worn to defend against negativity that is directed at you. Black stones have protective energies in the sense that black is the absence of light, and therefore, can be used to create invisibility.

- Fortifies self confidence and responsibility
- Sharpens your senses
- Encourages a healthy egotism

68 Opal Gemstone

Description: A form of silica where the arrangement of silica grains and water content (which can be up to 30%) results in the play of colour.

Enhances: intuition, inspiration, imagination, creativity, memory, psychic awareness, moderation of greed, emotional balance

Aids the maintenance or treatment of: eyesight, lungs, pineal and pituitary glands, heart

Special Features: Its animosity for greed and corruption make this a stone not to be used by the impure of heart.

Where to Wear: finger or throat

Chakra: Because it carries the full spectrum of colours, it can resonate with each chakra point.

Zodiac: Libra / Aquarius / Pisces / Cancer

Birthstone: October

Dream: great possessions

Care: Opals need to be treated with care. Some are sensitive to detergents and cosmetics. As they have a high water content, they can eventually dry out and crack. They should be immersed in water once a month and if stored, place with a drop of water in an unsealed plastic bag. Never wear while sun bathing, swimming or washing.

All of Nature's splendour seems to be reflected in the manifold opulence of fine Opals: fire and lightnings, all the colours of the rainbow and the soft shine of far seas. Australia is the classical country of origin. Almost ninety-five per cent of all fine opals come from the dry and remote outback deserts.

The group of fine Opals includes quite a number of wonderful gemstones, which share one characteristic: they shine and sparkle in a continually changing play of colours full of fantasy, which experts describe as "opalising".

Opals and emotions

For ages people have been believing in the healing power of Opal. It is reported to be able to solve depressions and to help its wearer find the true and real love. Opals are supposed to further enhance the positive characteristics for people born under the zodiac sign of Cancer. Black Opal is recommended to those born under Scorpio, and Boulder Opal is the lucky stone for Aries.

The fantastic colour play of Opal reflects changing emotions and moods of people. Fire and water, the sparkling images of Boulder Opal, the vivid light flashes of Black Opal or the soft shine of Milk Opal – striking contrasts characterise the colourful world of this fascinating gemstone. Maybe this is the reason why it depends on our daily mood which Opal we prefer. Opals are like human emotions: you always experience them different and anew.

Blue Opal

Blue Opal is a stone that will soothe erratic emotions and enhance personal courage.

- Enhances your ability to communicate what is in your heart
- Helps in overcoming those things you do to yourself that are harmful
- Strong connection to the sea and creatures of the sea (dolphins, mermaids, etc.)

The opal is said to be many things including the most powerful of healing stones, the stone of hope, the stone of great achievement and even the "stone of the Gods".

It is said to be the stone of love, but only to faithful lovers. The opal will bring misfortune to an unfaithful lover.

Fire opals are a fiery red-orange color. They are found in Brazil Hondurans and Mexico.

69 Peridot Gemstone

Description: Also known as Chrysolite, is a gem variety of Olivine and comes in a variety of green, from clear yellowy green to bottle green. A dark crystal can be lightened by heating.

Enhances: patience, mental and emotional clarity, happiness, sleep, confidence, balance emotions

Aids the maintenance or treatment of: stress, tissue regeneration, depression, cleansing organs, heart, digestion, jealousy, glandular system imbalance, muscles

Where to Wear: throat

Chakra: solar plexus / navel/heart

Zodiac: Libra / Leo / Capricorn

Birthstone: August

Care: Can be washed under luke warm water with a drop of detergent and water softener - rinse well in clear water as the soapy film can detract from the stone's lustre. Best to dry in the open air.

Peridot is mentioned in many ancient references as chrysolite. It is mentioned throughout the Bible, and early Christians considered it sacred. Today still, Catholic Bishops traditionally wear a ring of peridot and amethyst as a symbol of purity and morality.

The peridot was believed to be a stone of springtime by ancients who considered it a gift from Mother Nature.

Healing qualities of peridot

Peridot is a stone of lightness and beauty. Only spiritual or clear-minded persons should use peridot. The person with too many earthly problems will not be able to understand the beauty of the Peridot. The very spiritual can wear peridot in a necklace with the stone at the base of the throat to feel its soothing effect. Used in a necklace, peridot is a protector against negative emotions.Peridot has been known to have healing effect on the gall bladder and liver.

Sources of peridot

Peridot is a gem variety from the olivine mineral group. The bottle green color is called peridot. Yellowish green is chrysolite. Olive green is olivine. Sources of peridot include: St. John's Island (Egypt), United States (Arizona and Hawaii), Myanmar, Burma, Australia, Norway, South Africa and Brazil.

The vivid, slightly golden shimmering green of Peridot is the ideal gemstone colour to complement a light summertime outfit. This is no surprise – Peridot, after all, is assigned to the summer month of August.

The ancient Romans were already quite fond of the gemstone and coveted the brilliant green sparkle, which does not change either in artificial light. They already named the stone "Evening Emerald". Peridot is found in Europe in many medieval churches decorating several treasures, like, for example, in the Cologne Cathedral. In the era of Baroque the deep green gemstone experienced another short flourishing, before it became forgotten.

70 Rhodochrosite Gemstone

Rhodochrosite comes in a variety of shades from bright red to soft shades of pink, and opaque forms with swirling patterns. It is an excellent conductor of energy. Rhodochrosite in pink tones:

- soothes the heart
- stimulates warm feelings of love and compassion
- benefits the creative process
- promotes intuition

Healing properties of Rhodochrosite

Stimulates circulation and blood pressure, kidneys and reproductive organs.

Sources of Rhodochrosite

For years, Afghanistan was the only source of rhodochrosite. Other sources include Australia, Germany, South Africa, Yugoslavia, Romania and the United States.

Rhodonite Gemstone

Rhodonite soothes the nervous system. This gemstone vibrates with love. Just holding this gemstone promotes relaxation and brings a sense of well-being. This is a balance gemstone and is used to clear the psychic centers.

Rose Quartz Gemstone

Your marriage can have more sparkle and fire when you keep a rose quartz under your pillow. You will look younger too.

Rose quartz is known as the love stone. It helps the user feel a strong sense of self-worth, therefore being worth love. Rose quartz is the stone of universal love. It is also the stone of love in marriage. When worn in jewelry the wearer feels a sense of self-worth.

Healing properties of Rose Quartz

Rose Quartz has a gentle vibration of love for the owner. It gives inner peace and helps in all matters pertaining to love in all its forms. Rose Quartz opens the heart to love. It also helps as a rejuvenator to the skin. It is a lovely stone for a young person.

71 Red Tourmaline (Rubellite) Gemstone

Red Tourmaline or Rubellite, rekindles one's passion for life!

It vibrates a deep resonance with the heart chakra, going deeper than other heart stones. It has the potential to open you to love on many levels.

Rubellite makes an excellent gift to one's love partner because it fans the flames of passion. It also stimulates courage and inspiration to protect those that you love.

- Helps one overcome fears about abundance, survival or safety
- Balances the base and heart chakras
- Provides a connection with true abundance
- Aids in finding your inner courage and strength

Combining rubellite with other stones

To intensify the love energies of rubellite, use it with rose quartz, kunzite or rhodonite. For help with healing the physical heart, use rubellite with green tourmaline. To heal emotional wounds, combine rubellite with rhodochrosite.

Healing properties of Red Tourmaline - Rubellite

Rubellite helps balance the brain by keeping your emotions under your own control. It soothes the nervous system, helps to heal hysteria, depression and obsessive behaviour.

Tourmalines are an important mineral group that can be found in a variety of colors - black or schorl tourmaline, shades of red, pink, green, blue and what is known as watermelon tourmaline, which is a crystal with green on the outside and pink in the middle. The green tourmaline brings success.

72 Golden Rutilated Quartz

Quartz stones that contains mineral inclusions are called "rutilated quartz" or "sagenite", popularly known as Venus-hair stone. Rutiles are small needlelike crystals. These may be red, black or brassy yellow.

Golden rutilated quartz integrates energy at many levels. It heightens the energy of other quartz stones and is an important healing stone.

- Illuminates the soul
- Cleanses and energizes
- Removes barriers to spiritual growth
- Filters negative energy

Rutilated quartz is an excellent stone to use if you need to change your direction in life.

It soothes dark moods, offerring relief from fears, phobias and anxiety. The needle inclusions add intensity and transmission power to the crystal.

Healing properties of rutilated quartz

It is used to aid respiratory difficulties, regeneration of cells, flow of energy throughout the body. It is an excellent balancing stone for a sad or weak heart.

Sources of rutilated quartz

Quartz with rutile inclusions are found in Madagascar, Brazil, South Africa, India, Sri Lanka, Germany and Switzerland.

73 Red Rutilate Quartz

Description: A form of quartz that contains needlelike inclusions of rutile.

Enhances: life force, inspiration, problem solving, stability, insight, energy

Aids the maintenance or treatment of: .brain, depression, immunity, tissue regeneration, respiratory problems

Special Features: Often used well with beryl. **Where to Wear:** anywhere **Chakra:** all signs **Zodiac:** Gemini / Taurus

Care: Can be washed under luke warm water with a drop of detergent and water softener - rinse well in clear water as the soapy film can detract from the stone's lustre.

Quartz stones that contains mineral inclusions are called "rutilated quartz" or "sagenite", popularly known as Venus-hair stone. Rutiles are small needlelike crystals. These may be red, black or brassy yellow.

Red rutile (rutilated quartz):

- Brings new hope
- Acts as an anti-depressant
- Relief from anxiety, sexual problems related to tension
- Helps develop vision for the bigger picture

Red rutile is an energy stone. Wear it or place it on your altar while performing magic rituals to increase the power of your magic spells.

The needle inclusions add intensity and transmission power to the crystal. **Red rutilated quartz makes a powerful healing stone** for this reason.

Healing properties of rutilated quartz

It is used to aid respiratory difficulties, regeneration of cells, flow of energy throughout the body. It is an excellent balancing stone for a sad or weak heart.

Sources of rutilated quartz

Quartz with rutile inclusions are found in Madagascar, Brazil, South Africa, India, Sri Lanka, Germany and Switzerland.

74 Serpentine Gemstone

Serpentine gets its name from the word 'serpent' because it resembles the skin of a snake. It has been used since ancient times to guard against disease and sorcery.

Serpentine makes an **exceptional meditation stone**. It helps you to find inner peace. Serpentine was carried in ancient Assyria to request the gods and goddesses to provide double blessings. Nursing women used it to regulate their milk supply.

Some of the uses of serpentine include:

- Protection against poisonous creatures such as snakes, insects,
- Balances mood swings
- Encourages the ability to solve conflicts by peaceful means

Healing properties of Serpentine

Serpentine can be placed directly on the skin. It is an aid to kidney and stomach complaints, relaxes cramps and menstrual pain and helps women who are unable to reach orgasm due to tension.

Sources of Serpentine

Serpentine is found in New Zealand, China, Afghanistan, South Africa, USA, and England.

Smokey Quartz Gemstone

Smokey quartz is nature's stone of endurance. If you need a extra boost, carry a smokey quartz gemstone with you. It promotes:

- Personal pride and joy in living
- Creativity in business
- Opens the path for perception and learning

Healing properties of Smokey Quartz

Smokey Quartz is connected with the sounds of the universe. It makes you more aware of sounds including telepathic sounds. Smokey Quartz helps relieve depression.

75 Sodalite Gemstone

Description: Resembling, and often confused with Lazurite (Lapis Lazuli), Sodalite also has pyrites but has more of a pale violet colouring. It can even be found with green tints.

Enhances: spiritual awareness, communication, mental and visual clarity, balance male/female energies, courage, harmony, creative expression, meditation, objectivity, sleep

Aids the maintenance or treatment of: metabolism, blood pressure, fear, anxiety, Iymphatic/ endocrine systems, pancreas, emotionally related illnesses, cleansing organs, immunity

Special Features: Works well with clear quartz.

Where to Wear: earlobes, throat

Chakra: brow / throat

Zodiac: Sagittarius

Care: Crystals can be fragile.

Sodalite brings inner peace. Keep sodalite in your pockets and in every room of your house, so its peaceful properties will flow all around you.

Sodalite is a dark blue stone with white calcite interspersed. It is sometimes confused with lapis lazuli as it also has small specks of pyrite in it. The largest deposit of sodalite is in Brazil.

Sodalite is the stone of athletics, as it stimulates endurance. It is said sodalite will harmonize the inner being or the conscious and subconscious mind. Sodalite promotes peace and harmony. Sodalite is extra lucky for writers.

Healing properties of Sodalite

Sodalite is associated with the thyroid. It is perfect in a necklace. Wear it when you want to loose a few pounds. It helps in communicating and will give confidence to speak more.

76 Black Tourmaline Gemstone

Rub black tourmaline for luck and happiness. This is a powerful stone and a very lucky stone. When the tourmaline is rubbed it becomes charged with magnetic electricity and the luck intensifies.

Colored Tourmaline

Tourmaline is black, but also shades of red, pink, green, blue and what is known as watermelon tourmaline, which is a crystal with green on the outside and pink in the middle. The green tourmaline brings success. **The pink tourmaline** will bring love and friends. Tourmalated quartz aids peace of mind. It is found in many countries including Burma, United States, Brazil and Zimbabwe.

Healing properties of Black Tourmaline

Tourmaline uses differs as its colors differ. All colors are very powerful and it must be used carefully. Each person seems to react differently to Tourmaline. It has been used with intestinal problems, but only a healer should use it. The Tourmaline is not recommended to be used in jewelry. It can be carried for short periods of time. Black Tourmaline pushes all negativity away.

Green Tourmaline

All the tourmalines contain a wide scope of healing effects. The multi-colored tourmalines combine several qualities.

Green Tourmaline (also known as Verdelite) brings a joy for life. It promotes an appreciation for the many wonders that life has to offer. It encourages patience and openness, as well as sincere interest in fellow human beings.

The magical uses of this stone include the stimulation of creativity. It is also used to **attract money and success in business.**

Healing properties of green tourmaline

Green tourmaline strengthens the heart and offers detoxification effects.

77 Red Tourmaline (Rubellite) Gemstone

Red Tourmaline or Rubellite, rekindles one's passion for life!

It vibrates a deep resonance with the heart chakra, going deeper than other heart stones. It has the potential to open you to love on many levels.

Rubellite makes an excellent gift to one's love partner because it fans the flames of passion. It also stimulates courage and inspiration to protect those that you love.

- Helps one overcome fears about abundance, survival or safety
- Balances the base and heart chakras
- Provides a connection with true abundance
- Aids in finding your inner courage and strength

Combining rubellite with other stones

To intensify the love energies of rubellite, use it with rose quartz, kunzite or rhodonite. For help with healing the physical heart, use rubellite with green tourmaline. To heal emotional wounds, combine rubellite with rhodochrosite.

Healing properties of Red Tourmaline - Rubellite

Rubellite helps balance the brain by keeping your emotions under your own control. It soothes the nervous system, helps to heal hysteria, depression and obsessive behaviour.

Tourmalines are an important mineral group that can be found in a variety of colors - black or schorl tourmaline, shades of red, pink, green, blue and what is known as watermelon tourmaline, which is a crystal with green on the outside and pink in the middle. The green tourmaline brings success.

78 Tourmalated Quartz Gemstone

Description: A form of clear quartz that has inclusions of black tourmaline crystals.

Enhances: balance of male and female energies, overerall balance, self confidence, meditation

Aids the maintenance or treatment of: negative emotions, chakra blockages, nervousness, lymphatic and digestive systems, endocrine system

Where to Wear: anywhere

Chakra: all chakras especially crown

Zodiac: all signs especially Libra

Care: Can be washed under luke warm water with a drop of detergent and water softener - rinse well in clear water as the soapy film can detract from the stone's lustre.

This super lucky stone has the luck of both the quartz and tourmaline. The luck in this stone is so strong it is recommended to carry one only for a short amount of time. It is best kept in a safe place and rubbed when powerful luck is needed.

Healing properties of Tourmalated Quartz

Tourmalated Quartz is clear or milky Quartz with black Tourmaline needles. This powerful stone should only be used by professional healers.

79 Gems For Relationship

.ove makes the world go round! Perhaps this is the year you will iscover true love. Or you will give love like never before and reap he true rewards. Or you'll open your heart to the joys of giving love n a selfless, unconditional way. Gemisphere would like to invite you o take a look at the ten special Love & Relationship gems guaranteed o make your heart a little warmer, your life a little brighter.

f you want to open your heart to more love, or have had difficulties vith love, or want to heal that broken heart once and for all, now is he time! Gemisphere offers these ten necklaces guaranteed to help ou create the love that makes hearts sing and the sun shine more rightly - a gift you can give yourself or someone you truly care about.

Ruby: Healing the Emotions

Radiant Ruby opens the heart and reveals divine love at the core of very molecule in creation. Become a vehicle through which divine ove can enter your life and touch all those around you. Powerful, eautiful, amazing Ruby!

Ruby Dream : Healing the Emotions

his dream of a necklace fulfills the mission of Ruby. It opens your eart to divine love and helps resolves love-related karma swiftly and asily. What a true and special gift!!

Ruby Rose : Healing the Heart

f you've ever had a broken heart, Ruby Rose will call to you. This entle necklace heals the wounds of lifetimes of pain, as it soothes, nends and strengthens the heart. Release the heaviness and help your eart find better balance with this lovely gift of Ruby.

Radiant Heart : Finding Inner Peace

Build the inner strength and awaken the most tender and playful part of you! This lovely blessing nurtures, heals and comforts you while it repairs and rebuilds any part of your emotional foundation that needs strengthening.

Roselle : Purifying the Emotions

Emotional limitations take flight in the presence of purifying Roselle. Now you can have the personal growth and happiness that comes with the release of emotional limitations and suppressed feelings. Let the love flow with rare, natural pink Roselle.

Rhodochrosite : Developing Inner Freedom

If love were a storm, it would be Rhodochrosite! This gentle tempest of a gemstone sweeps away any negative patterns and emotional clutter that could hold you back from your own natural brilliance. Rhodochrosite has the power to help you transform your life and truly become the being of love you are meant to be.

Magic Gift : Self-Worth

The wholeness of love and self-confidence combine as one in this magical necklace. Powerful Ruby and transforming Rhodochrosite join forces in Magic Gift to increase self-love and let your spiritual essence shine through. A gift indeed!

Libra : Balanced Change

Transformational Rhodochrosite is accelerated by the rainbow energy of Quartz. As your overall energy is raised, all life signifies your beauty and brings you to a new level of appreciation for all you have to give. Welcome the joys that change can bring.

Rhodonite : Emotional Transformation

Where is a kind word when you need it? Where is a soothing touch and healing heart? It is all right here with the miracle of Rhodonite. Instantly soothing and uplifting, Rhodonite transforms your emotional foundation and lifts you up where you belong!

Mother of Pearl : Stirring Primordial Memory

Let the divine love flow through you and fill every need you have ever had. Sweet, dear Mother of Pearl delivers every promise she makes! Listen to the song that divine love sings to your heart though the magic of Mother of Pearl.

80 Gems For Physical Healing And Purification

The primary focus of some therapeutic gemstone necklaces is physica healing. Working with these gemstones can deeply purify and heal the physical body, help release toxins and negative energies stored in the organs, and support immune and endocrine systems. Except for Quartz, these gemstones are predominantly green.

The therapeutic necklaces for physical healing and purification can help an individual:

- Resolve a chronic or acute illness
- Experience more energy and vitality
- Relieve chronic pain
- Strengthen a weakened organ
- Boost the immune system
- Soothe the body after trauma or surgery The therapeutic gemstone necklaces that focus on physical healing and purification include:

Quartz : Attracting Life Force
Emerald: Healing the Physical Body
Summer : Healing the Physical Body
Dark Green : Aventurine Purifying the Physical Body
Dark Green Emerine: Physical Healing and Purification
Light Green : Aventurine Uplifting the Physical Body
Light Green Emerine: Soothing the Physical Body
Malachite: Harmonizing the Body
Patience: Here and Now
Bloodstone: Strengthening The Immune System.

81 Gems For Karmic Healing And Resolution

The primary focus of some therapeutic gemstones is the healing of karmic patterns. Working with these gems can help transform negative behavior patterns, break bad habits, and eliminate destructive relationship dynamics. They can also help resolve the negative patterns from the past that perpetuate physical or mental conditions. These gemstones are predominantly orange.

These therapeutic gemstones can help you:

- Stop self-destructive habits, such as smoking or overeating
- Climb out of a rut
- Develop new, healthier ways of relating to others
- Eliminate behavior patterns underlying an unwanted physical condition
- Break free of a pattern of destructive relationships

The therapeutic gemstone necklaces that focus on karmic healing and resolution include:

Rhodochrosite: Developing Inner Freedom

Magic Gift: Self-Worth

Libra: Balanced Change

Carnelian: Revitalizing Your Being

Opalight: Resolving Karma.

Gems For Mental Clarity And Expansion

Mental healing is the primary focus of some therapeutic gemstones. Working with these gems can expand mental potential, clear the mind and increase one's ability to focus, and help heal certain mental imbalances. These gemstones are predominantly blue.

These therapeutic gemstones can help you:

- Experience greater mental clarity
- Focus more easily
- Clear out mental "garbage"
- Improve memory
- Expand the mind to its full potential Resolve a chronic or acute illness

Therapeutic gemstone necklaces that focus on mental clarity and expansion include:

Aquamarine: Illumination
Blue Sapphire: Healing the Mind
Lavender Fire : Healing the Mind
Inner Quest : Opening to the Blue Ray
Angelfire : Purifying the Higher Mind
Lapis Lazuli : Harmonizing Heart and Mind
Pharaoh : Resolving Egyptian Karma
True Self : Confidence
Sodalight : Purifying the Aura
Blue Phoenix : Rebirth
Lavender Light : Clearing the Mind.

83 Gems For Spiritual Awakening

The primary focus of some therapeutic gemstones is the development and awakening of higher consciousness. Working with these gemstones will help open spiritual awareness, abolish impediments to higher states of consciousness, and strengthen intuition. Except for Citrine, these gemstones are predominantly indigo and purple.

These therapeutic gemstones can help you:

- Let go of certain attachments
- Develop "inner" hearing
- Open to higher states of consciousness
- Strengthen and clarify intuition
- Accelerate spiritual growth through color ray healing

Therapeutic gemstone necklaces that focus on higher consciousness and spiritual awakening include:

Indigo : Developing Intuition

Lavender : Awakening to Soul

Amethyst : Attaining Wisdom

Purple Ray : Letting Go of Attachments

Insight :True Meaning of Wealth

Breanna : Higher Consciousness

Purple Eagle : Multi-Dimensional Healing

Fluorite Rainbow & Light Stream : Color-Ray Healing

Lavender Rainbow : Color-Ray Nourishment

Ocean Rainbow : Color-Ray Nourishment

Citrine : Fulfilling Your Potential.

84 Gems For Masculine Healing and Empowerment

The primary focus of these two gemstones is restoring balance between one's masculine and feminine aspects. These gemstones can restore self-confidence and physical vigor, help resolve relationship issues, and repair endocrine imbalances.

These therapeutic gemstones can help you:

For women

- Empower their feminine nature
- Improve fertility
- Resolve a gynecological condition
- Relieve menstrual cramps

For Men

- Empower their masculine nature
- Improve physical endurance
- Experience more courage, vigor, and vitality
- Resolve an endocrine imbalance
- Enhance sexual prowess

For both men and women

- Strengthen and tone the reproductive system
- Restore or create harmony with a mate
- Protect oneself from other people's negative thoughts and feelings.

Therapeutic gemstone necklaces that focus on masculine and **feminine healing and empowerment include:**

Green Tourmaline

Balancing the Male

Pink Tourmaline

Balancing the Female

Rubelle

Balancing the Female.

85

Gems For Healing And Nourishing With Earth Energies

This special class of therapeutic gemstones includes opaque gemstones whose primary focus is healing, energizing, and nourishing the physical body. In general, the colors of these gemstones are muted, earthy, and variegated.

These therapeutic gemstones can help you:

- Attract whatever the physical body needs for healing
- Feel more grounded and stable
- Accelerate the positive effects of other therapies
- Integrate the effects of other life-giving therapies
- Develop healthier personal boundaries

Therapeutic gemstone necklaces that focus on healing and nourishing with Earth energies include:

Agate : Nature's Nourishing Energies

Leopardskin Jasper p: Attracting Beneficial Influences

Golden Leopard : Supporting Inner Transformation

Leopard Magic : Integrating the Body

Poppy Jasper : Enlivening your Body

Quartzite : Anchoring Positive Change

Riverstone : Accelerating Change

Onyx : Becoming Grounded

Mother of Pearl: Stirring Primordial Memory.

86 Colour Ray Healing With Seven Special Gemstones

The Earth's gems play a surprisingly central role in how color functions, not only in the mineral kingdom but in life itself. This role has far-reaching implications for the healing arts, therapy, and energy medicine. Indeed, the subject of color healing is such a significant part of gemstone energy medicine that it deserves several books of its own. Thus, what follows is simply a brief introduction to this vast topic.

Color rays are the most fundamental building blocks of all living things. Just as visible light is comprised of the seven colors of the rainbow, so is the life force - the force that enlivens, sustains, and nourishes everything that lives. We human beings are manifestations of this vital force. Thus, at the deepest level we too are made up of spectrums of these seven color rays.

Each color ray has a specific purpose, and all seven color rays are essential for life. Being continually supplied with and nourished by a proper balance of color rays is essential to every aspect of health. In an optimally healthy person, all seven colors are present in balance. Any deviation from that balance moves a person away from ideal health and an optimal expression of life - and will ultimately lead to disease and disharmony.

Certain special gemstones can help us correct such color-ray imbalances and begin to help us heal and grow in the deepest way possible.

Seven Color Ray Gemstones

All therapeutic gems embody intense concentrations of energy. They help remove obstructions to the flow of life force in our bodies and being. Seven of these gemstones also serve another, very special function: each of them carries one of the seven color rays of the life force. Embodied in the crystalline matrix of each of these seven gems is the pure and highly concentrated vibration of a certain color ray.

Because the color rays themselves are not physically tangible, it is difficult to work with them directly in their pure form. The gemstones that carry the seven color rays solve this problem. They are the Earth's most powerful tools available for drawing the color rays from their origins through one's inner dimensions, or subtle bodies, to the physical body. Indeed, these seven gemstones are the Earth's premier color healing tools.

The seven color ray gemstones and the color rays they carry are: Ruby (red ray), Carnelian (orange ray), Citrine (yellow ray), Emerald (green ray), Blue Sapphire (blue ray), Indigo (indigo ray), and Amethyst (purple/violet ray).

Each of these gemstones not only contains the concentrated energy of a certain color ray; each also acts as a magnet to continuously draw a current of that color to the physical plane from its unlimited source, the pure life force that lies at the basis of all life. When you wear a necklace of a color ray gemstone, you effectively step into the current of color that the gemstone draws to itself.

As this current moves through your subtle bodies to your physical body, any blockages in your being associated with that color ray are washed away in the current. For example, when you wear a therapeutic Emerald necklace, your entire being is flooded with the green color ray. The green ray helps neutralize the disharmonies that cause physical disease, particularly those centered in the organs. As blockages to the green ray dissolve, any excess of green ray in the body and aura is relieved, and any deficiency of green is filled by the abundant influx of green ray. Through this mechanism, wearing a color-ray gemstone necklace can have profound implications for your life and health at the deepest levels.

Through this mechanism, wearing a color-ray gemstone necklace can have profound implications for one's life and health at the deepest levels.

Healing the Physical Body with Color

Each of the seven color rays is particularly healing and nourishing to a certain system in the physical body. For this reason, one can greatly benefit a particular system by wearing its corresponding color ray necklace. For example, the red ray nourishes and supports the muscles, tendons, and fascia. Consequently, wearing Ruby can help strengthen these parts and resolve certain conditions related to them.

The following chart lists the color rays, the color ray gemstones, and the physical systems that are nourished and supported by each color ray.

Color Rays and Physical Systems

Color Ray	Gemstone	Physical Systems
Red	Ruby	Muscular system (muscles, tendons, and fascia)
Orange	Carnelian	Lymphatic systemSoft connective tissueEndocrine system (glands)Adipose tissue
Yellow	Citrine	Organs of elimination (skin, bladder, urinary tract, kidneys, intestines, and eliminative aspects of the liver)
Green	Emerald	Organs in the torsoBrain*
Blue	Blue Sapphire	Vascular systemNerve sheathsCerebrospinal fluidSense organsBloodBrain*
Indigo	Indigo	Skeletal system (bones, ligaments, joints, and cartilage)
Purple/Violet	Amethyst	Nerve cellsBrain*

*Note that the brain, which serves many functions, is associated with several color rays.

Therapeutic gemstones are jewels of multidimensional healing and transformation - gifts from the Earth waiting to be opened. To enjoy these gifts, we need only know how to unwrap and use them; yet, doing so can be a very simple matter. By shaping therapeutic gems into spheres and stringing them into necklaces, we can tap their vast healing potential and reap their far-reaching therapeutic benefits.

87 Care Of Gemstones

Like all expressions of life, gemstones need and deserve care to retain their vitality. As therapeutic gemstones help us release energetic impurities and blockages, some of these released energies cling to the surface of the gemstones. These disharmonious energies quickly build up on the surface of the gems, inhibiting their ability to work at peak capacity. Regular cleansing clears these energies and restores the gemstones to their naturally vibrant state. Several minutes of care given regularly will keep therapeutic gemstones vital and ready to help us take our next step in growth and healing.

Basic Care Guidelines

When using a therapeutic gemstone necklace regularly, cleanse it at least two to three times a week using one of the following methods: Water Rinse, Salt Bed, Plant Rejuvenation, or Sunbath (see descriptions below).

When not in use, store cleansed gemstones in a drawer, covered container, or jewelry roll.

Handle all therapeutic gemstones with care. Some are particularly fragile, such as Purple Rainbow Fluorite, Malachite, Mother of Pearl, and Rhodochrosite. They naturally break, scratch, and chip more easily than other gemstones.

To Be Avoided

Avoid storing gemstones near strong electromagnetic fields, such as those emitted by televisions and computers, which can disrupt the gemstones' energies.

Avoid exposing gemstones to x-rays, such as at the dentist, in a hospital, or at an airport security station. X-rays will be absorbed by the gemstones and released later into the user's aura.

Avoid wearing gemstones in chlorinated swimming pools or hot tubs. Chlorine weakens natural-fiber thread and adversely affects the surface of certain gems.

Avoid smoking and wearing synthetic perfume when wearing therapeutic gemstones, especially porous stones. The fumes can interfere with the free flow of a gemstone's energy.

To Protect The Thread's Longevity

Do not wear necklaces longer than 20 inches to bed. Instead, lay them within three feet of your body.

During intense physical activity, such as jogging, remove your necklace and place it in a secure pocket.

In general, be sure that the thread is completely dry before wearing or storing a necklace. For example, you can rinse a necklace before you go to bed and leave it flat to dry within three feet of your body while you sleep.

Four Cleansing Methods

Any of the four methods described below can cleanse therapeutic gems of the disharmonious energies they tend to collect during use. For certain gemstones, some methods are more appropriate than others; these special considerations are noted where required.

Water Rinse - Two to three times a week, or more often as needed

Rinsing gemstones in alternating hot and cold running water gently shocks the gems into releasing their accumulated energies and then washes these energies away. Hold the entire necklace under hot running tap water for about 5-10 seconds and then immediately switch to cold running water for 5-10 seconds. Repeat this process three to five times. To ensure that the hot water doesn't become too hot, which can cause some gems to crack, test the temperature with your fingers; if the water is too hot for your fingers, it may be too hot for the gems. If you are going to wear the necklace immediately after cleansing it, end the rinse with hot water; otherwise, end with cold water.

After rinsing, pat the gems dry with a soft cloth or towel. Unless there's an immediate need to place the necklace around your neck, lay it flat for at least several hours to allow the thread to dry completely. Putting a necklace with wet thread around one's neck can stretch and weaken the thread.

Special considerations: Rinsing will dull the polish of Rhodochrosite, Lapis Lazuli, Malachite, Sodalight, Indigo, and Mother of Pearl. Therefore, use other cleansing methods for these gems.

Every three to four weeks: For gemstones that tolerate rinsing, occasionally use a small amount of mild, non-synthetic soap to remove body oils from the surface of the gems.

Salt Bed - Two to three times a week, or more often as needed

Sea salt absorbs the disharmonious energies that accumulate on the surface of therapeutic gems. Before going to sleep for the night, lay the gemstones in a dish or bowl of sea salt, directly on the salt. If possible, place the dish within three feet of your bed to maintain the gems' energetic connection with your aura. Replace the salt about every two weeks.

Plant Rejuvenation - Two to three times a week, or more often as needed

Plants generate a living energy field that can absorb and transform the disharmonious energies we release. At the end of the day, wrap the gemstone necklace around the base of a healthy houseplant, or lay the necklace in its branches. If possible, place the plant within three feet of your bed to maintain the gems' energetic connection with your aura. During the night, the gemstones will be gently cleared of any accumulated energies. For a deeper cleansing and rejuvenation, place the gemstones outside underneath or in the branches of a shrub or tree for several days.

Sunbath - Every one to two weeks, or more often as needed

Sunlight provides the deepest cleansing of any in-home method. Sunshine clears, energizes, and revitalizes therapeutic gems. Unless the gems are water-sensitive, first rinse them in hot and cold running water as described above. Then lay the gems in direct sunlight for up to one hour. Ideally, expose the gems to the sun directly, rather than through a glass windowpane. If possible, lay the gems directly on the earth, grass (preferably untreated), or branches of a plant. On a cloudy day, gems can be left in the sun for two to three hours. Avoid excessive exposure to the sun, since this has a negative effect similar to that of sunburn on human beings.

Cleansing Guidelines For Individual Gemstones

The chart below provides gem-specific details for the Water Rinse and Sunbath methods described above. Special Care notes indicate additional needs of certain gems.

Gemstone	Water Rinse Details	Sunbath Maximum Time	Special Care
Agate	2 – 3 times a week	1 hour	
Amethyst	Every day for the first two weeks of constant use. Thereafter, 2 – 3 times a week.	30 minutes	
Aquamarine	2 – 3 times a week	5 minutes	
Bloodstone	2 – 3 times a week	1 hour	

Blue Sapphire 2 – 3 times a week 1 hour

Carnelian Every day for the first two weeks of constant use. Thereafter, at least 2 – 3 times a week. 1 hour Store in closed container to counteract its tendency to pick up unwanted energies from the atmosphere.

Citrine 2 – 3 times a week.Begin with a long cold rinse, and always end with cold water. 5 minutes Alternative: Place in snow.

Dark Green Aventurine Every day for the first two weeks of constant use. Thereafter, 2 – 3 times a week. 15 minutes Alternative: Place on grass in rain for minimum of 30 minutes.

Emerald 2 – 3 times a week 1 hour

Green Tourmaline 2 – 3 times a week 1 hour

Indigo Avoid rinsing. Rinsing dulls polish. 5 minutes Wipe with a soft cloth 2 – 3 times a week.Alternative: Place in moonlight.

Lapis Lazuli Avoid rinsing. Rinsing dulls polish. 30 minutes Wipe with a soft cloth 2 – 3 times a week.

Lavender 2 – 3 times a week 1 hour

Leopardskin Jasper 2 – 3 times a week 30 minutes

Light Green Aventurine Every day for the first two weeks of constant use. Thereafter, 2 – 3 times a week. 15 minutes Alternative: Place on grass in rain for minimum of 15 minutes.

Malachite Avoid rinsing. Rinsing dulls polish. 30 minutes Wipe with a soft cloth 2 – 3 times a week.

Mother of Pearl Avoid rinsing. Rinsing dulls polish. 1 5 minutes Wipe with a soft cloth 2 – 3 times a week.

Onyx 2 – 3 times a week 1 hour

Opalight 2 – 3 times a week 1 hour

Pink Tourmaline 2 – 3 times a week 1 hour

Poppy Jasper 2 – 3 times a week 1 hour

Purple Rainbow Fluorite Avoid rinsing. Rinsing dulls polish. 15 minutes Wipe with a soft cloth 2 – 3 times a week.Store separately to prevent scratching and breakage.

Quartz Every day for the first two weeks of constant use. Thereafter, 2 – 3 times a week. 1 hour Occasionally wash with mild natural soap to remove body oils and restore frosted appearance.

Quartzite Avoid rinsing. 1 hour Wipe with a soft cloth 2 – 3 times a week.

Rhodochrosite Avoid rinsing. Rinsing dulls polish. 1 hour Wipe with a soft cloth 2 – 3 times a week.Store separately to prevent scratching and breakage.

Rhodonite 2 – 3 times a week 1 hour

Riverstone 2 – 3 times a week 1 hour

Roselle Every day for the first two weeks of constant use. Thereafter, 2 – 3 times a week. 5 minutes

Ruby 2 – 3 times a week 1 hour

Sodalight Avoid rinsing. Rinsing dulls polish. 5 minutes Wipe with a soft cloth 2 – 3 times a week.Avoid contact with plastic; Sodalight absorbs gases released by it.

Enhancing Your Sensitivity to Gemstone Energy

The Gemstone Guardians feel it is essential for all of us to develop sensitivity to the energies and effects of our gemstones. By observing our gems before and after cleansing, we will become more aware of the difference between gemstones that have shut down because of energetic stress-and those vibrant with light and sound.

88 Star Signs

Aquarius Jan 21 - Feb 20 air
aquamarine / chrysoprase / garnet / jet / labradorite / lapis lazuli / opal/silver

Pisces Feb 21 - Mar 20 water
amethyst / aquamarine / chrysoprase / fluorite / labradorite / moonstone / opal/pearl/silver /

Aries Mar 21 - Apr 20 fire
agate / amethyst / carnelian / coral/diamond / garnet / obsidian / ruby / sapphire / topaz

Taurus Apr 21 - Mar 20 earth
aquamarine / chrysocolla / emerald jade / kunzite / lapis lazuli / rose quartz / rutilated quartz / rhodonite / selenite / turquoise

Gemini Mar 21 - Jun120 air
agate / aventurine / chrysocolla / chrysoprase / pearl/ rutilated quartz / sapphire / staurolite / topaz

Cancer Jun 21 -]ul 22 water
amazonite / chrysoprase / emerald / moonstone / opal/pearl

Leo Ju1 23 - Aug 22 fire
agate / amber / aventurine / carnelian / chrysocolla / citrine / diamond / garnet / obsidian / peridot / pyrite / topaz / ruby

Virgo Aug 23- Sep 22 Earth
agate / amazonite / amber /aventurine / carnelian / chrysocolla / citrine / jade / jasper / obsidian / rose quartz / sapphire / zircon

Libra Sept23-Oet22 air
aquamarine / chrysoprase / coral / kunzite lapis lazuli / moonstone / opal/peridot / tourmalinated quartz / sapphire / red/pink tourmaline / turquoise

Scorpio Oet 23 - Nov 22 water

aquamarine / citrine / emerald / garnet / kunzite / malachite / moonstone / ruby / green tourmaline

Sagittarius Nov 23 - Dee 22 fire

amethyst / azurite / lapis lazuli / labradorite / sodalite / topaz / red/pink tourmaline / zircon

Capricorn Dee 22 - Jan 20 earth

amber / amethyst / capricorn / garnet / haematite / jet / labradorite / obsidian / onyx / peridot / ruby / sapphire / tiger's eye / green tourmaline

All signs bloodstone / jade / clear quartz / smoky quartz / tourmalinated quartz / colourless tourmaline

SYMBOLISM

Agate	health and long life
Amazonite	creativity & personal expression
Amber	memory
Amethyst	sincerity
Aquamarine	tranquility
Aventurine	luck stone
Azurite	abilities of the mind
Bloodstone	courage
Carnelian	contentment
Chrysocolla	feminine stone joy
Chrysoprase	balance
Citrine	clarity of mind
Copper	energy flow
Coral	understanding
Diamond	the stone of the mind
Emerald	love
Fluorite	fortitude
Garnet	constancy
Gold	affection

Haematite	courage
Jade	friendship and confidence in love
Jasper	endurance
Jet	calm
Kunzite	feminine stone
Labradorite	protection
Lapis Lazuli	rebirth
Malachite	inner awareness
Moonstone	warmth and friendship
Obsidian	wisdom
Onyx	inspiration
Opal	hope
Pearl	grace
Peridot	happiness
Pyrite	intellect
Clear Quartz	energy purifier
Rose Quartz	love
Rutilated Quartz	rebirth
Smoky Quartz	mental clarity
Tourmalinated Quartz	balance
Rhodonite	confidence
Ruby	humility and pureness of spirit
Sapphire	truth and wisdom
Selenite	awareness
Silver	purity
Sodalite	truth
S1aurolite	well-being
Tiger's Eye	energy flow
Topaz	fidelity
Tounnaline	communication
Turquoise	prosperity
Zircon	energy.

89 Country of Origin

Agate	Brazil, India, Uruguay, China
Amazonite	Brazil, India, Madagascar, USSR
Amber	Baltic Region, Denmark, Norway
Amethyst	Brazil, Madagascar, India, USSR
Aquamarine	Brazil, Madagascar, USSR, USA
Aventurine	Urals, Siberia, Tibet, India, Brazil
Azurite	Australia, Greece, France, Chile
Bloodstone	India, Urals, Australia, Brazil, China
Carnelian	USSR, Arabia, Egypt, Brazil, India
Chrysocolla	Chile, Peru, USSR, Zaire, USA
Chrysoprase	Poland, Urals, USA, Australia
Citrine	Brazil, France, Madagascar, USSR
Copper	USA, Chile, Germany, Mexico
Coral	Mediteranean, Pacific, Indian Ocean
Diamond	South Africa, Australia
Emerald	Colombia, Russia, Zambia, Zimbabwe
Fluorite	Switzerland, Norway, England
Garnet	South Africa, USA, Siberia, Italy
Gold	Transvaal, Australia, Canada, PNG
Haematite	Angola, Canada, Russia, Brazil
Jade	Burma, China, Tibet, South America
Jasper	India, Urals, Brazil, Italy, France
Jet	England, Spain, France
Kunzite	Brazil, Madagascar, USA
Labradorite	Canada, Scandinavia, USA, Italy
Lapis Lazuli	Afghanistan, Chile, Russia
Malachite	Zaire, Zambia, USSR, Australia

Moonstone	Australia, Burma, India, Tanzania
Obsidian	Iceland, Hungary, Italy, Mexico
Onyx	Brazil, India, Uruguay, China
Opal	Australia, Czechoslovakia
Pearl	Australia, Indian Ocean, Persian Gulf
Peridot	Zebirget (Red Sea), Hawaii, USA
Pyrite	Italy, Spain, USA, Elba, Sweden
Clear / Rose Quartz	Brazil, Madagascar, Italy
Rutilated Quartz	Alps, Australia, Polar Urals
Tourmalinated Quartz	Alps, Australia, Polar Urals
Smoky Quartz	Brazil, Madagascar, Alps
Rhodonite	Canada, Russia, Sweden, Australia
Ruby	Burma
Sapphire	Kashmir
Selenite	UK, France, Russia, USA
Silver	Norway, Australia, Canada, Chile
Sodalite	Canada, USA, USSR, Austria, Italy
Stauralite	Switzerland, France, USA, England
Tiger's Eye	South Africa, Australia, Burma, India
Topaz	Brazil, USSR, Germany, Nigeria
Tourmaline	Brazil, Sri Lanka, Madagascar, USA
Turquoise	Iran, USA, Siberia, France
Zircon	Cambodia, Sri Lanka, Thailand, USA

Quick guide to healing & enhancement properties

Anxiety	aventurine, citrine, sodalite
Arthritis	chrysocolla, copper, coral, flourite, garnet, malachite, topaz, turquoise
Backache	carnelian, emerald, fluorite, haematite, sapphire

Blood Circulation	amethyst, aventurine, azurite, bloodstone, carnelian, chrysocolla, copper, fluorite, garnet, gold, haematite, jasper, kunzite, malachite, opal, pearl, peridot, pyrite, rose quartz, ruby, silver, sodalite, staurolite, topaz, turquoise
Blood Detoxification	gold, haematite, tiger's eye
Blood Pressure	(high)chrysoprase, emerald, jade
Bones	aventurine, azurite, chrysocolla, fluorite, onyx, rhodonite, selenite
Bronchial System	amber, bloodstone, haematite, jet, kunzite, pearl, rutilated quartz, turquoise
Cleansing Organs	amethyst, aquamarine, bloodstone, copper, coral, jade, lapis lazuli, moonstone, peridot, rose & smoky quartz, ruby, sodalite, topaz, zircon
Communication	amazonite, chrysocolla, coral, sapphire, sodalite, tiger's eye, tourmaline, turquoise
Concentration	fluorite, onyx, selenite
Confidence	agate, carnelian. citrine. garnet, gold, moonstone, topaz, tourmaline
Courage	agate, amethyst, bloodstone, carnelian, diamond, emerald, garnet, haematite, lapis lazuli, sodalite, staurolite
Depression	bloodstone, carnelian, chrysoprase, coral, emerald, jade, jasper. jet. onyx, pyrite, rutilated & smoky quartz, sapphire. selenite, topaz, zircon
Digestive System	agate, aquamarine, chrysocolla. coral, gold. jade, jasper, lapis lazuli, obsidian. pearl, peridot. pyrite, rhodonite. tiger's eye, *Topaz,* tourmaline, tourmalinated quartz

Emotional Balance	agate, amazonite, aventurine, chrysocolla, coral, emerald, gold, jade, jasper, jet, Kunzite, lapis lazuli. moonstone, onyx, opal, peridot, clear & smoky quartz. silver, topaz, zircon
Endocrine System	amethyst, sodalite, tourmaline
Energy Negative	(removal) citrine, jade, jet, obsidian, rose quartz, topaz, tourmaline, turquoise
Energy Positive	agate. haematite, ruby, rutilated quartz, selenite
Eves	aquamarine, aventurine. diamond, lapis lazuli, obsidian, opal, sapphire, tiger's eye, turquoise
Fertility	chrysoprase, emerald, rose & smoky, quartz silver
Fluid	jade, moonstone
Headache	amethyst, aventurine, haematite, jet, pearl, rose quartz, turquoise
Hormonal Balance	gold, moonstone, silver
Immune System	amethyst, copper, emerald, jasper, lapis lazuli, rutilated quartz, rhodonite, sodalite staurolite
Imagination	opal
Lymphatic System	labradorite, moonstone, sodalite, tourmaline, tourmalinated quartz
Male/Female Balance	moonstone, onyx, sodalite
Meditation	amethyst, azurite, carnelian, emerald, garnet, clear quartz, sapphire, sodalite, tiger's eye
Memory	amber, amethyst, carnelian, chrysoprase, emerald, jade, opal, pyrite, rhodonite tourmaline

Menopause	diamond
Mental Balance	aventurine, azurite, bloodstone, chrysoprase, copper, coral, emerald, jasper, kunzite, lapis lazuli, sapphire
Mental Clarity	amazonite, aventurine, azurite, bloodstone, carnelian, chrysoprase, coral, diamond, jasper, peridot, selenite, silver, sodalite, zircon
Mental Disorders	coral, fluorite, garnet, kunzite, malachite
Metabolism	chrysocolla, copper, soda, topaz
Motivation	carnelian, citrine, copper ruby
Nerves (calm)	aquamarine, selenite, tourmaline
Patience	garnet, labradorite, malachite, peridot
Pancreas	rhodonite, sodalite, tiger's eye
Physical Balance	agate, amazonite, aventurine, chrysoprase, copper, coral,.emerald, jasper, kunzite, is lazuli, sapphire
Psychic Abilities	azurite,emerald, fluorite, lapis lazuli, moonstone, opal, smoky quartz, turquoise, sodalite
Pineal Gland	amethyst, azurite, malachite, opal,clear quartz, zircon
Pituitary Gland	amethyst, azurite, malachite, moonstone, opal, clear quartz, rhodonite, zircon
Relaxation	amber, amethyst, copper, emerald, jade, jet, kunzite, malachite, smoky quartz, topaz, tourmaline
Rheumatism	chrysocolla, coral, fluorite, garnet, malachite, turquoise
eproductive organs	carnelian, moonstone, rose & smoky quartz
Sexual Balance	agate, diamond, onyx, rose quartz

Sleep	azurite, garnet, jet, malachite, moonstone, peridot, ruby, soda, topaz, tourmaline, zircon
Stress	amber, chrysocolla, chrysoprase, fluorite, haematite, malachite, obsidian, onyx, pearl, peridot, rose quartz
Strength	citrine, copper, diamond, garnet, haematite, kunzite, rhodonite, zircon
Tissue Regeneration	azurite, carnelian, gold, kunzite, malachite, peridot, rutilated & smoky quartz, turquoise
Throat	amber, topaz
Violence	(moderation of) bloodstone
YinNang Balance	aventurine, onyx, chrysoprase, tiger's eye

♦ ♦ ♦ ♦

Other Books on
OCCULT SCIENCE

1.	Lotus Horoscope **(New)**	195/-
2.	Teach Yourself Vaastu **(New)**	175/-
3.	Reiki The Science of Healing	175/-
4.	The Marvels of Palmistry	125/-
5.	Healing Power of Gems	195/-
6.	Awake Kundalini	160/-
7.	Learn Meditation	125/-
8.	Teach Yourself Numerology	125/-
9.	Teach Yourself Astrology	125/-
10.	Teach Yourself Graphology	160/-
11.	Teach Yourself Effectively Feng Shui	160/-